To Bob

Best Wishes!

Bob Kennett

TAKING THE VOODOO
OUT OF ECONOMICS

by
Robert J. Genetski

REGNERY BOOKS

CHICAGO • LAKE BLUFF • NEW YORK

Regnery Books is an imprint of Regnery Gateway,
Inc. All inquiries concerning this book should be
directed to Regnery Gateway, Inc., 950 North Shore
Drive, Lake Bluff, IL 60044.

ISBN:-0-89526-588-5
Library of Congress Cataloging in Publication
Number: 86-6586

Introduction and Acknowledgements

Many years ago, while struggling through graduate school, I turned to one of my classmates and asked if he knew what this subject—economics—was all about.

"That's silly," he replied, "We're both getting excellent grades, so we both must know what it's about."

"No," I said, "I'm not questioning whether we can remember what we hear in class or repeat what's written in our books, I'm just wondering if anyone really understands this subject."

"Oh, I see what you mean," he said, while thoughtfully staring into space. After a while he looked back at me and said, "I have no idea what they're talking about. I wonder if anyone does?"

Many years have passed since that discussion, but I still remember it as if it were yesterday. Throughout my career, both in academia and in the business world, I have retained mixed emotions toward my fellow economists. On occasion I have stood in awe of the brilliance of their analysis, while at other times I found myself embarrassed by their foolishness. Although the main purpose of this book is to make me rich and famous, there is another objective. I hope to resolve some of the more obvious causes of confusion in a subject that's too important to be left to the experts.

In acknowledging those who have enabled me to complete this project the list is long. First, I have to extend my gratitude to my Creator, to Adam and Eve, my grandparents and more recently my parents, Alex and Helen. Next in line is my high school guidance counselor who advised me not to attend college since it would simply be a waste of time and money. Although some who read this book will wish I had taken his advice, a sufficient number of years has passed for me to conclude that he was mistaken. More than anything else, this one incident left me with a healthy skepticism regarding how much the "experts" in any field really know.

Throughout my career I have been fortunate to have encountered bright, imaginative people who have not hesitated to question and challenge my beliefs, forcing me to adjust and delve ever deeper in my quest for knowledge. Among those who have been particularly helpful in this regard are Jude Wanniski, Milton Friedman, Art Laffer, Beryl Sprinkel, Dismas Kalcic, Richard Rahn, Alan Reynolds, Debra Bredael, Brian Wesbury, and Nancy Wesselius. Needless to say, I alone am responsible for any voodoo that may remain in my own analysis.

Finally, my family insists that they be named. My wife, Maureen, as well as Bob, Dennis, Alexis and Tom, probably don't realize how much they have actually contributed. Their loving support along with periodic family squabbles have kept me close to earth and made all the extra effort worthwhile.

Contents

Chapter

Contents

Book 3 Key Topics in Economics

Book 1

Approaching Economics

Chapter 1

Voodoo Overview

In the heat of the 1980 Republican Presidential primary George Bush referred to Ronald Reagan's economic ideas as voodoo economics. Subsequently, he regretted his statement and called it "one of the dumbest things I've ever said." Whatever the merit of the original charge, it provided the basis for identifying a school of economics that has been practiced without the benefit of a legitimate title for quite some time. With its new-found label, Voodoo Economics will no longer be relegated to obscurity. Instead, its prominence among competing schools of thought must be recognized.

Most schools of economic thought are fairly easy to define so long as generalities take precedence over specifics. Voodoo economics is no exception. Given current usage, it can be defined generally as any objectionable economic view or policy. Needless to say, this is a fairly subjective definition. Since the definition of legitimate economic analysis varies, one person's wisdom and insight are often another's voodoo. If voodoo economics is ever to achieve recognition as a meaningful school of thought, it has to be defined more objectively. It may be viewed as any school of economic thought characterized by inconsistent analysis and incomprehensible statements—one that relies on incantations as opposed to logic and generally tends to ignore or defy evidence contrary to its views. The best way to identify voodoo thought is to distinguish it from legitimate, honest-to-goodness economic analysis.

At first glance, this may appear to be an impossible task. It is not. There is a rich tradition of economic thought that has been refined over hundreds of years as some of the greatest minds pondered the workings of the economy. When the insights provided by this tradition are supported by evidence, none dare call it voodoo!

However, if tradition is so rich, so insightful, why does apparent confusion—so much voodoo—surround economics? The reason is simple. Confusion and voodoo *appear* to permeate the subject because they *do* permeate the subject. And there are many good reasons why. One is economists themselves. They are a strange lot, and some of their idiosyncrasies serve to encourage the arcane and primitive practice. The nature of these idiosyncrasies and how they contribute to the practice of voodoo are discussed in Chapter 2. A second reason stems from the approach that economists take in teaching economics. The organization of most economic texts inadvertently contributes to confusion and thereby promotes voodoo reasoning. Chapter 3 explains why this is so and offers some general principles to avoid such pitfalls.

In order to identify voodoo economics, it is first necessary to understand how the rich tradition of economic thought relates to some of today's key issues. Chapter 4 works to achieve this objective. It begins by applying some general principles of organization in explaining how the economy works. The objective is to structure this broad topic in such a way that an incessant stream of information can be categorized sensibly. Once the appropriate structure has been determined, competing theories, personal experiences and other relevant information can be readily filed for easy reference.

After establishing the structure, it is necessary to begin to add substance. This is done in Chapters 5-14. Building on the prescribed guidelines, the first step is to understand the topic or issue at hand. Issues such as growth and prosperity, business cycles or price stability often mean different things to different people. A great deal of confusion and potential voodoo can be avoided by a thorough understanding of the topic being considered. Once this has been accomplished, different views or theories, as well as evidence, can be evaluated.

In considering different theories, it is useful to begin with some historical perspective. For hundreds of years economists have tried to solve the secrets of growth, prosperity, business cycles and inflation. Progress in understanding these subjects has come at an uneven pace. Insights are often carefully developed by one generation of thinkers, only to be discarded and then rediscovered by a new generation. It is fascinating to realize how many of the basic ideas in economics were first presented several hundred years ago.

Philosophers throughout the ages have contributed to our present understanding of how the economy works. Their contributions are often ignored in the search for "new ideas." This is a mistake. Time and again, the evidence suggests that many of the traditional views long-held by economists contain much wisdom. As such, these views should form the starting point of any effort to determine how the economy works. Revolutionary new explanations are seldom actually new or revolutionary. Rather, they are often vestiges of some primitive branch of thought that has long since proved extinct.

Chapters 15-18 deal with some of the key economic issues of today—deficits, interest rates, international influences, and the morality of economic systems. With some topics, such as deficits and interest rates, applying a systematic approach to the issues quickly reveals that much of what has been written recently on these topics is in the finest traditions of voodoo thought.

Many economists have taken a strong dislike to the title. Some have even stated that they would like to keep the voodoo in economics! However, keeping the public confused is in the best interests of neither the profession nor society as a whole. A widespread understanding of basic economic forces and their impact is important for the well-being of all people. Also, some economists have suggested that quotes and names of specific individuals should be used to illustrate the use of voodoo. However, the objective is not to name economic witchdoctors, for the names change from year to year and from generation to generation. Rather, the purpose is to identify a way of thinking. Once this is done, the practitioners of voodoo, both present and future, will readily identify themselves.

In its entirety, this book has several objectives. One is to provide a firm foundation for understanding what might otherwise appear to be hopelessly complex issues. With this foundation and the accompanying evidence, it should become easier to distinguish legitimate economic analysis from voodoo. A second objective is to make economic issues clear and comprehensible to the non-economist. These issues affect not only our standard of living, but those of our children as well. As a result, they are far too important to be left in the hands of economists. A final objective is to impress upon the reader the fact that learning economics is a continual process. No one can achieve a working knowledge of the subject by simply reading books. Events must be observed as they unfold. By providing a frame of reference for such observations, this book represents the first stage in what must be an on-going attempt to understand the economic forces affecting our lives.

Chapter 2

Does Anyone Understand Those Economists?

Although it would be nice to begin by tackling some of the great issues of the day, the first order of business is not to understand any great issue, but to understand economists. Of course, if you're married to an economist, you surely know enough to skip this chapter. However, if you aren't that lucky, the following may help explain many economists' idiosyncrasies. Understanding economists is necessary for several reasons: first, they need understanding; second, their idiosyncrasies can inadvertently contribute to the practice of voodoo economics; and finally, they are the ones we often must rely on for insight into the workings of the economy.

To begin, we should realize that there are two extreme views regarding professional economists. Some people view economists as gods who understand all the boundless complexities of the economic universe....Seriously!...Most of the people with this view are economists themselves. Others view economists as a confused and irrelevant lot with little practical information to offer. This group includes many who have tried to rely on economists for making critical decisions. While neither of these extreme perceptions is accurate, each contains some elements of truth.

Such extreme attitudes towards economists develop because of the implication of their subject for each individual's well-being. Economics deals with factors that influence our income and wealth, and—what can be even more interesting —the income and wealth of our neighbors. Understanding the forces of economics involves understanding what creates jobs and what destroys them, what sends stock prices soaring or interest rates tumbling. Consequently, understanding the forces of economics involves understanding the forces that determine our living standard—our lifestyle. And any change in economic policies will have implications, not only for our own living standards, but for the difference between ours and our neighbor's, and between our own and those of our children. With so much at stake, it's no wonder that a proposed change in economic policies can incite passions in those who understand its consequences.

Unfortunately, while economics has great potential importance, it too often turns out to be a boring, confusing, useless subject. Much of the blame for this state of affairs rests with economists themselves. Economics is not only a complex subject, but one in which the realm of professional opinion regarding specific issues is often in a state of flux. This is just one reason it can be so difficult to get straightforward, consistent answers to some of the most fundamental economic questions. There is a standing truism about the economics profession that only economists can truly appreciate: economic professors need not change exam questions from year to year to prevent cheating; although the questions may remain the same, the appropriate answers are always changing.

The major questions do, essentially, remain the same: How does the economy operate? Why do some economies prosper while others wither? What determines the distribution of wealth and income? What causes economic booms, recessions, and depressions? Where does inflation come from? And what causes interest rates to behave the way they do? The questions are easy, the answers difficult. Interestingly, many economists can answer these questions correctly in the abstract. The difficulty emerges when the questions are placed in the context of actual events.

Classroom vs. The Real World

Economists quickly concede how difficult it is to understand what is actually happening in any economy, much less to predict the future. Perhaps the most intriguing statement in this regard came from a well-known Harvard economist who once told a reporter,"Present developments are so uncertain that just about anything could possibly happen, and it probably will." Not to be outdone, a famous economist with the prestigious Brookings Institution summarized his daring forecast for 1983 by concluding that "there may or may not be an economic recovery."

One fundamental reason for economists' difficulty in providing coherent, consistent comments on actual events stems from the complexities associated with the real world. In the classroom, economists can simulate a laboratory experiment by assuming that the only thing to change is the one factor they are considering. Upon entering the real world, all the other factors are continually changing. As a result, it becomes very difficult to comment on the real-world impact of a particular policy, since its impact may be overwhelmed by other factors. Furthermore, real-world policies are always changing. Therefore, any analysis must not only incorporate how the economy works, but also an in-depth knowledge of relevant policy changes and a thorough assessment of their immediate and longer-term impact. When classroom economists apply their analysis to the real world without recognizing these factors, the first hints of voodoo begin to appear.

Fields of Expertise

The field of economics covers an incredibly wide range of subjects. Many of the most learned economists have spent relatively small proportions of their professional time studying the issues considered so important to most of the public. Even so, the temptation to comment on popular issues is so great that most economists succumb, regardless of their field of expertise or their familiarity with the relevant evidence.

When experts make statements outside their field, they no longer carry the authority of an expert. In 1983 the Nobel Prize in economics went to Professor Gerard Debreu, a specialist in mathematical economics. During a press conference following the Nobel announcement, reporters asked Professor Debreu what he thought of the nation's present economic policies. He immediately disappointed reporters by stating that his work wasn't directly related to current policies and therefore he would not comment. Unfortunately, this noble position is seldom taken by an economist, particularly a Nobel economist.

Careless and Meaningless Statements

Economists also confuse many issues by making careless and meaningless statements. For example, it is often stated that the consumer holds the key to economic trends—if the consumer decides to spend lavishly, the economy will become stronger; if not, the economy will be weak. This statement is one of the most common—and also one of the most meaningless—ever made. Technically, it is not wrong. Since close to two-thirds of all spending is done by consumers, no meaningful increase in economic activity can occur without them. Undoubtedly, the consumer is crucial! But to state that strength or weakness in the economy will depend on what the consumer will do is to state the obvious. The relevant issue is not what consumers will do, but what will *cause* them to do it. Such careless or meaningless statements can be minimized by focusing on the factor that initiates change as opposed to the change itself.

Time Horizons

The time horizon provides another source of potential confusion for economists and those seeking their aid. A policy or action usually has one effect immediately, another after a brief period of time has passed, and still another over the long haul. Economists often find themselves in heated disagreement over the impact of a policy simply because someone forgot to specify the time period involved. For example, imagine the following question on an economics exam:

Placing an effective ceiling on the price of a product will lead to:

a) a lower price than would otherwise exist
b) the same price as would otherwise exist
c) a higher price than would otherwise exist

Each answer is either correct or incorrect, depending upon the time period under consideration. In the first instance, price controls can lead to a lower price than would have existed. However, at the artificially lower price, people will want more of the item than at the higher price. Also, producers who are being paid less for their product will cut back on production. In this sense, the price controls create pressures for a shortage of the item. Hence, the effective price will rise as people have to wait in line for the product, or purchase it at inflated prices on the black market. Once the controls have done sufficient damage, the black market price (or if controls are removed, the actual price) will tend to be higher than it ever would have been without controls. At the higher price, production will increase and demand will be reduced. Given enough time, the price will settle in at where it would have been without the controls. To complicate matters further, the length of time for these adjustments will be substantially different depending upon the nature of the item being affected. Now, try asking the next economist you meet what effect price controls have on prices—it can tell you a lot about that economist's views on the importance of time. When economists present their conclusions regarding policies without referring to the time horizon, the result tends to be more voodoo than substance.

Bias and Prejudice

Another reason for disagreement among economists concerns individual bias and prejudice. As do many people, economists often have strong views about how the world should be. At times, these views dominate their analysis and policy prescriptions. For example, a few professional

economists favor price controls. Although their recommendations for controls are usually offered as a solution to higher
prices, their real concern is the impact of higher prices on
the poor. They feel a moral obligation to help the poor, or
at least to redistribute income away from the rich, and they
formulate their analysis and policy prescriptions in ways
aimed at accomplishing this objective.

With important political and moral implications hanging
on each policy prescription, economists are tempted to in-
ject their personal moral biases into their analysis. This is a
sad mistake. If an individual wishes to be a moralist, he should
proclaim himself as such and not try to manipulate economic
reasoning. For economics in and of itself has major implications for issues of morality. Predetermining those issues and
allowing those biases to influence the economic debate does
a disservice not just to economics, but also to the moralists
and spiritual leaders. Such leaders want and need good economic input to assist them in resolving moral issues. If a certain set of policies avoided immediate relief to the poor in
exchange for developing a highly productive working class
some years later, society's moral leaders must know as much
as possible about the economic implications of these policies in order to make a more informed judgment about their
morality.

Owing to the complex and highly charged nature of their
work, economists' statements must be analyzed closely for
some common, but less substantive, sources of confusion.
If economists are not careful in specifying their assumptions
or the time period implied in their analysis, or if they do not
reflect on whether their statements contain their personal
biases, then their statements and conclusions can be very misleading. Since it is often difficult for economists to elaborate
on all these factors, observers must be aware that such factors not only exist, but they can play an important role in turning reasonable analysis into voodoo.

Chapter 3

S-I-T-E-O
A Five-Step Approach To
Understanding Economic Issues

As with any complex subject, economics becomes more comprehensible if various topics are approached and categorized in a systematic way. Such an approach involves five steps: 1) establish a structure or frame of reference for organizing material, 2) identify each topic or issue, 3) choose a theory to explain each topic, 4) review the evidence and 5) observe developments. For short, this five step approach to economic issues is referred to as S-I-T-E-O:

> **S**tructure
> **I**dentity
> **T**heory
> **E**vidence
> **O**bservation

Establishing the Structure

The human mind is capable of absorbing an enormous amount of information, but to do so efficiently, the mind must categorize new material effectively. One of the most inefficient ways to learn is to read an encyclopedia from beginning to end. Without the ability to categorize new information in some systematic order, most information will be quickly forgotten. In attempting to master any complex subject, it is necessary to begin with a systematic approach—one that enables us to categorize new information quickly and efficiently so that it can be understood and retained. For example, instead of beginning the study of medicine with all topics starting with the letter "A," you should start with a clear over-view of the basic functions of a healthy body. After this is mastered, subtopics dealing with ailments, bone structure, or the major organs might be developed. Once such cate-gories are established, a doctor who comes across a fairly com-plicated case can place it in its appropriate field and either review the relevant literature or direct his patient to the proper expert.

The appropriate structure, or filing system, accomplishes several objectives. It enables the student of any subject to isolate attention on particular issues, to recognize how the issue at hand relates to others, and to focus attention on the most substantive issues.

The best structure is usually unknown to those trying to learn about a new field. Usually only those thoroughly familiar with the field can provide guidance concerning an appropriate structure. If the appropriate guidance is provided, learning in that field can proceed at an accelerated pace. Without the appropriate guidance, learning can be a slow, painful and often unproductive process. Whatever the subject, the first step in mastering it is to discover the structure that provides both a useful overview of the field as well as a helpful frame of reference for classifying and subclassifying important subjects.

Identify the Issue

Once the structure has been determined, the next step is to identify the issues at hand. Again using the field of medi-cine as an example, the issue may be fairly broad (how the body functions) or relatively narrow (what causes athlete's foot). Whatever the issue, identifying it is the first critical step to fruitful inquiry. In economics the issue may consist of how a healthy economy works—how it grows and prospers—or it may deal with an illness—inflation.

As a general rule, when first investigating a subject you should attempt to master broad issues. Once the big picture, or overview, of the subject is obtained, the role of subtopics often can be viewed in a clearer perspective. In many cases, knowledge of the broader topic is prerequisite to understanding the subtopic. In this regard, one particular issue—interest rates—is among the most interesting and complicated in all of economics. It would be self-defeating to begin an inquiry into economics by raising the issue of *what* determines interest rates. Understanding interest rates involves first understanding growth, inflation and business cycles, and then mastering the concepts of money, saving and credit along with a host of other factors. Whatever the order of topics, the first step toward an intelligible inquiry is to identify the object of inquiry, understand it thoroughly and recognize where it fits into the scheme of things.

Choosing a Theory

Once the issue has been identified, it must be explained. This is the most critical part of the approach. It involves choosing a theory or framework that captures the essential aspect of the issue being considered. A good framework will be sufficiently simple so as to be readily understood, flexible enough to incorporate further advances in knowledge, and durable enough to withstand the test of time. The framework may consist of a highly speculative theory or an established fact, depending upon how far knowledge has advanced.

Returning to the field of medicine, the issue under consideration may be how a healthy body functions, and the theory might consist of viewing the body as a group of living cells whose nourishment is supplied by the flow of blood which is controlled by the heart. If the theory is essentially correct, additional studies and tests should help to confirm the theory's implications for disease, malfunction and treatment. While this basic theory for analysis of the body is accepted today as fact, it was not always so. The practice of bloodletting was based on an alternate (and largely incorrect) framework for understanding how the body functions. In medicine as in economics, a bad theory can result in a misleading analysis with potentially deadly results.

Economics is a unique science. Knowledge has not advanced sufficiently to consider many explanations as facts.

Instead, almost all issues in economics involve choosing a theory to explain a certain phenomenon. A theory represents a simple explanation of a complex issue. Understanding almost any aspect of economics often qualifies as a complex problem. A realistic picture of any economic event involves considering hundreds of thousands of different factors, all of which are interrelated. No one can possibly deal with this degree of complexity. As a result, theories are developed.

Theories attempt to explain some event by focusing on a limited number of factors. If the influence of the particular factors chosen tends to dominate all other factors in explaining the event, then the theory is good. If the factors chosen are not the dominant ones, the theory is bad. A good theory enables us to predict the results of different forces. Not only will a good theory identify the dominant forces contributing to an event, but also the forces on which a theory focuses must be those that *initiate* a change in the system. The complete theory traces the impact of these forces to show just how they influence the event under consideration.

For instance, if a change in tax rates leads to a whole range of adjustments in the economy, then the tax change represents the initiating force. It must be clearly identified as such, and its effects must be viewed as the result of the tax change. If a reduction in taxes leads to greater economic activity, then the increase in activity, along with any other ramifications, should be viewed as a consequence of the tax change. In this case, logical reasoning can proceed to a justifiable conclusion. In a similar vein, an increase in the money supply may first lead to lower interest rates. The lower rates may stimulate business and then produce higher interest rates. Again, by clearly identifying the dominant, initiating cause of a change in economic pressures, logical reasoning can produce a conclusion.

In contrast, a failure to identify the initiating force can lead to circular reasoning. If someone were to suggest a theory stating that lower interest rates stimulate business activity while higher interest rates produce a slowdown in activity, the analysis would soon become hopelessly confused. If lower rates stimulate business, the stimulus would produce higher rates that would slow business, thereby producing lower rates that would...and so on forever. The mistake in this reasoning is the failure to identify an appropriate starting point. Interest rates do not change unless something causes the change. Many different factors can bring about such change. As we will see in Chapter 16, without clearly identifying the cause of a change in interest rates, it's impossible to say anything meaningful about subsequent developments.

A similar mistake is frequently made regarding the impact of budget deficits. Some argue that a slowdown in business activity increases the federal budget deficit, while the deficit stimulates business activity. Hence, larger deficits stimulate business activity. But that would lead to smaller deficits, which in turn would slow activity and thereby lead to higher deficits. Once again, the analysis has no beginning and therefore no logical conclusion. The problem is that changes in a budget deficit can result from any number of different things, many of which will affect the economy in different ways. Without specifying the specific reason for the change in the deficit, it is impossible to say anything meaningful about its impact. Failure to identify specifically the initiating cause of an economic event signals the presence of voodoo.

While more than one factor can be considered as providing the impetus for change, it is important to limit the theory to those factors that dominate the analysis. This is often difficult when dealing with economic issues, since everything affects everything else. When any one factor influencing an economy is changed, it sends reverberations through the entire economy. As a result, it is tempting to try to mention all factors that might have an impact on the issue at hand. The problem is that it is virtually impossible to consider everything or even all things that might be important. While everything does affect everything else, the interrelationship among different elements in the economy is so hopelessly complex that any all-encompassing framework is doomed to fail. The key to understanding economics is to be highly selective in isolating the dominant forces that are causing other factors to change. Once those forces have been isolated, attention can be directed toward increasing knowledge about their operation and impact.

Even when the initiating cause is appropriately identified, there are problems choosing the best theory. Economists do have legitimate differences of opinion over which theory best explains an event. However, it is instructive to recognize the ephemeral nature of some of these views. At times, certain ideas or theories dominate economic thinking. Then ideas change, and alternative theories reign supreme. The failure of consistent, well-established theories to remain in vogue has led to much confusion.

The nature of some economists' convictions is highlighted by some statements made by an aging graduate-school professor. He defended his (Keynesian) views that changes in psychology were the key to understanding business cycles. When several students questioned both the logic and evidence behind his views and compared them with some alternative (monetarist) views, he proceeded to relate his experience with economic theories. "You must understand," he patiently explained to the class, "I was a monetarist before many of you were born. Even after Keynes wrote during the Great Depression, I remained a monetarist. In the late forties and early fifties, when most economists had become Keynesians, I remained a loyal monetarist. Finally, in the late fifties I was persuaded to become a Keynesian—and, very frankly, I'm too old to change back now."

Notice the implication of this statement. Those educated early in the professor's career were taught that the economy operated one way. Those exposed to the same man later in his career were taught that it operated another way. Nor is this professor unique. Most college students educated in the fifties and sixties learned their economics from a single, popular textbook. As theories changed during these years, so did the famous text's explanation of how the economy worked. The edition that was popular in earlier years bore little relation to the edition published in the late seventies. Here again, the specific theories taught to a generation of college students were often dependent, not upon the belief of a particular teacher, but upon the particular edition of a certain textbook.

In a sense, economics had developed a creative obsolescence which seemed to assure that the conventional wisdom of the day soon would be replaced by a new and different view of how the economy operated.

The changes in economic theories mirrored in conventional texts did not necessarily reflect any particular economist's belief. Often, well-known economists held steadfastly to their own views of how the economy operated. At the University of Chicago, instruction reflected Milton Friedman's belief that the money supply was the key factor in explaining business cycles. At Yale (and most Ivy League schools), the Keynesian views prevailed, with psychology viewed as the key to understanding business cycles. One of the most fascinating phenomena was that of equally bright students entering different colleges only to emerge with totally different beliefs about how the economy worked.

A truly amazing thing is that the development of ideas of how the economy operates continues right up to the present time. As recently as the late 1970s, the conventional view of federal deficits was that they stimulated spending and led to an increase in business activity. In the early 1980s, the conventional wisdom flip-flopped. Federal deficits began to be viewed as something that would raise interest rates and stifle business activity instead of promoting it. This development has to be extremely confusing to a student who learned his economic theory in the mid-1970s, only to find that it had become obsolete within a relatively short time span. According to the conventional wisdom, answers that were correct in the mid-1970s were suddenly incorrect in the early 1980s.

Moreover, we can rest assured that this state of confusion will persist in the future. Today's graduate schools are apparently determined to stay one step ahead of a confused public. Recently, an economics professor at the University of Chicago was asked if the department was still teaching students that the behavior of the money supply was a major factor influencing the economy, now that Milton Friedman, the chief proponent of that view, had retired.

"Oh, heavens no!" the professor replied. "We've progressed beyond that. We now teach them that neither the money supply nor the federal budget has an important effect on the economy.''

Nor is the impact of money or the budget the only issue where confusion appears to have free reign. Does an increase in the money supply lead to lower or higher interest rates? Is inflation good or bad for stocks? Is a strong dollar a good development for an economy, or is it bad? Although the questions remain the same, the answers keep changing.

If the correct answers to key economic questions did change every few years, economics would be a hopelessly complex subject, understood only by those with divine revelation. Fortunately, the correct answers do not change. Through the ages, the response to basic economic forces has remained the same. Those students who are fortunate enough to be taught about how these forces operate do not find their knowledge of economics becoming obsolete every few years.

Great economists of the past often have unraveled the apparent mysteries surrounding these basic forces, only to have their work ignored by future generations. As a result, economists often find themselves grappling anew with issues that long ago had been resolved. In economics, as in so many fields, the most significant progress can often be made, not so much through the many bold and revolutionary new ideas that are always emerging, but by not forgetting what has already been learned. For most issues in economics, the appropriate theory has long since been clearly and effectively presented. The theories chosen in this book are neither new nor unique. Each has roots deeply entwined in the rich history of economic thought.

Still, even a theory that has been around for centuries is not necessarily appropriate. For neither the reasonableness of the theory nor its heritage can insure that it is correct. Moreover, a theory that is appropriate for one time and place may be inappropriate for another. Critical to choosing the correct theory is evaluating the relevant evidence as best we can. The greater the body of evidence in support of a particular theory, the more confidence we can have that it will provide a useful analysis. However, as with so many issues in economics, the nature of evidence is often mysterious. As such, we should consider some of the issues surrounding economic evidence.

Evidence

You may wonder what economists can prove about how the economy operates. The answer is straightforward— nothing! Laboratory scientists often can provide proof of the influence of a certain factor by holding all others constant. Economists don't have this luxury. Hence, it is impossible to be completely certain of the mechanics of the economy. For this reason, the search for information about how the economy operates is a never-ending venture...one that begins with a theory.

The confidence we attach to any particular theory will depend on many factors. At the outset, our level of confidence in a theory will depend on our existing knowledge of the subject. All of our subsequent experience, studies and observations should be geared toward adjusting that confidence. Information that supports the theory will help convince us that we are on the right track. Information that is inconsistent will reduce our confidence.

Before an evaluation of the evidence can be made, it is useful to define what constitutes valid evidence. For many economists, evidence consists of relating two or more series of data by using a wide range of very precise statistical and mathematical tools. This procedure, which goes by the highly sophisticated term *econometrics*, has been widely used to develop ''evidence'' to support various economic propositions.

Unfortunately, in spite of (or perhaps because of) sophisticated statistical techniques, much of the evidence produced by econometric studies has been useless. One famous study by a widely-respected economist indicated that social security taxes caused a decline in savings, a reasonable proposition. After receiving widespread praise, it was discovered that a programming error had been made. Once the error was corrected, the same statistical techniques suggested the opposite conclusion, which even the economist doing the study felt was completely unreasonable.[1] Had it not been for the accidental discovery of this error, the study would still be used today as "evidence" regarding the impact of social security on saving.

In another case, two widely respected economists showed that during the 1960s large federal deficits tended to be related to higher interest rates. When the same relationship was updated with information from the 1970s, it suggested that higher deficits were related to lower interest rates![2]

In still another instance the shifting of "evidence" from one side to the other is reminiscent of the flight of a tennis ball.

> ...Barrow and Niskanen found no significant link between annual M1 growth and the deficit over the post-World War II period. But it was a fickle finding, being reversed when Hamburger and Zwick performed the exercise.... This result in turn was reversed when McMillan and Beard used revised GNP data in the calculations. It was reversed once again when Hamburger and Zwick again redid their work.[3]

Unfortunately, these studies are fairly typical of the "evidence" that many professional economic journals publish regarding economic issues. There are numerous reasons for the shortcomings in what passes for economic evidence. One problem is the data. In many cases the data represent only a rough guide to the concept that economists are dealing with. Too often, developing more appropriate data becomes a major project in itself, one that is seldom pursued. The end result is that highly sophisticated statistical tools are often applied to highly inadequate data.

A second reason for problems in econometric analysis is the use of the wrong theory. All of the data manipulations and computer runs in the world cannot help to advance our understanding if the underlying explanation of a certain phenomenon is incorrect.

A more specific problem is the widely held view that it is improper to try to relate one key element to another—such as taxes to growth, or money creation to inflation. Many economists believe that, since the economy is complex, they must attempt to incorporate that complexity into their analysis. Unfortunately, there is no way this can be accomplished. The operation of the economy is, in fact, so complex that its behavior can never be fully explained by any economic model. Attempts to do so by plugging a handful of factors into an equation often lead to a false sense of security that all the correct factors have been identified and measured appropriately. In most cases, neither of these crucial objectives will have been fulfilled.

This is not meant to imply that all statistical studies are worthless. Numerous studies undertaken by capable researchers have added significantly to our understanding of how the economy functions. However, it is often difficult even for experts to determine the merit or confidence that should be attached to particular studies. Referees and editors of economic articles are often very capable at tracing through the logic, reasoning and appropriateness of the statistical tools used to shed light on a particular problem. But they are often inadequately prepared to evaluate either the theory or data being used. Too often, the end result is an extremely clever—often brilliant—use of statistical techniques that is hastily applied to the wrong theory, inadequate data, or both. Few researchers follow the example of Milton Friedman and Anna Schwartz who, when faced with the question of the impact of money on the economy, spent more than a decade developing historical data on the money supply. Still fewer are aware of the limitations that remain even after the most painstaking and scholarly efforts have been used to refine the data.

Although economists can never prove anything about how the economy operates, substantial progress has been made in understanding the pressures and forces at work in any economy. Much of this understanding is not new. It developed gradually over the past few centuries as some of history's greatest thinkers focused their attention on economic issues. Unfortunately, economists too often neglect these historical insights and march off attempting to rediscover the proverbial wheel. For this reason it is important to be aware of historical developments in the field and to recognize when they are being ignored.

Finally, never hesitate to strip away the complexities and look at the relevant evidence. If someone suggests that rapid increases in the money supply tend to be the main cause of price increases, look at the historical patterns. See for yourself the extent to which this may or may not have been true. If someone else argues that tax cuts have been an important factor leading to periods of prosperity, ask for the evidence. When were taxes cut? From what levels? When did prosperity exist? Armed with this information, anyone can begin to make informed judgments about the evidence surrounding key economic issues.

Observation

The final step in our systematic approach is observation. Yogi Berra, the famous catcher and manager for the New York Yankees, once remarked that "you can observe a lot just by watching." Since new fads and theories are always popping up and old ones may lose their usefulness (or simply be wrong), it is necessary to observe and test each explanation continually. Diligent studies, the passage of time and continued keen attention to economic developments will provide the appropriate evidence for strengthening or weakening our confidence in any particular theory.

These, then, are the five steps to a systematic approach to economic issues: develop the structure, identify the issue, choose a theory, evaluate the evidence, and—as Yogi suggests—observe. To obtain a working knowledge of economics, the work is never really done. Now, it is time to use this approach to investigate the broad issue of how the economy operates.

Book 2

How the Economy Operates

Chapter 4

How The Economy Works
Applying S-I-T-E-O

U nderstanding the operation of an economy is an unwieldy process. The guidelines established in the previous chapter are helpful in making it wieldy. First, establish a structure for organizing the material. Second, clearly identify each topic in the structure. Third, introduce a theory to explain each topic. Fourth, review the evidence regarding the theory. And fifth, observe. Use ongoing observations to raise or lower the confidence placed in a particular theory.

Establishing the Structure

To be effective, the structure used to organize issues should enable us to isolate our attention on specific issues while providing an overview to understanding the operation of basic economic forces. As such, we must separate the broad topic—how an economy operates—into major subtopics.

Dissecting a broad topic such as this into subtopics is not unique. Most modern economics books develop a structure based on who does the spending in the economy and what they buy. Hence, consumers represent one subtopic, investors another, government still another, and the rest of the world rounds out the picture. However, this type of structure directs our attention away from the most important forces at work in an economy. Consequently, its main effect is to confuse rather than to enlighten.

Discovering the source of economic resources for purchasing is far more important than finding out who makes the purchases. In other words, what are the initiating forces that lead to the creation of wealth? And, far more important than what is purchased is the impact of the purchase on the economy. In other words, what are the initiating forces that determine how much is spent and what it will buy? It is more useful to develop a structure that focuses on how the economy performs rather than on issues such as who spent what, on what. In a T.V. soap opera, it can be fascinating to try to determine who is having an affair with whom. However, preoccupation with such details can divert us from the more important, more substantive issues. Likewise, in an effort to focus on the more substantive economics issues, the structure used here consists of three topics: growth and prosperity, business cycles and the value of money.

The development of an economy—its long-term growth path—represents the first topic. Since the forces affecting development tend to change gradually over time, it is useful to distinguish these factors from those that affect short-term swings in business activity. Such short-term shifts are called business cycles—the second topic in our structure. The final topic deals with the value of money: what money is worth and why it may be worth more, less, or even become worthless.

As mentioned above, everything in economics affects everything else. Just as the fuel, engine and driver all interact to influence the way a car operates, so it is with economic factors. Although the forces influencing growth and prosperity tend to change slowly over time, they can undergo such a dramatic change that the consequences actually dominate short-term swings in the economy. China's move toward freer markets in the late 1970s reportedly led to a doubling in China's income in five years. Under such circumstances, a major structural improvement can dominate all other forces and produce what appears to be a cyclical boom, but in fact is a lasting move toward prosperity.

Similarly, cyclical forces can be muted for so long that the economy experiences an extended period of stability. Such a development occurred during the 1960s when the U.S.

economy went for almost a decade without experiencing a serious downturn. Just as the forces affecting the long-term behavior of the economy can influence short-term swings, those influencing short-term swings in the economy can affect its long-term behavior. And, to top it off, the value of money can influence both of these factors and be influenced by them. In spite of these complications, the distinction surrounding the forces influencing long-term growth, short-term swings in the economy and the value of money is both valid and important, particularly for establishing a useful structure. The fact that the fuel, engine and driver all interact to move the car doesn't stop us from focusing our attention separately on any one of these factors. In fact, it is only our ability to focus solely on the engine, without considering the fuel or the driver, that makes it possible for us to begin to understand how the car operates.

Identifying Topics

The meaning of growth and prosperity, business cycles and the value of money is often confusing. When people start off with different ideas regarding what constitutes prosperity, a business cycle, or the value of money, any economic discussion soon turns to babble. As a result, it is important to describe carefully the issue at hand. This is done in the following chapters as each of the topics are presented.

Choosing the Appropriate Theory

Once the topics are identified, they must be explained. The explanation involves choosing a theory that isolates the dominant, initiating force that explains the issue at hand. In the case of growth and prosperity the task is nothing less than identifying what it is that contributes to the development of an economy. For business cycles, the appropriate theory will identify the dominant, initiating cause of short-term swings in business activity. And, with respect to the value of money, the appropriate theory will correctly identify the major force that determines what money is worth.

Initially, it may appear that this is an overly ambitious task. How could any one book assume to have the answers to such important questions? Aren't there countless theories offered in each of these areas?...Before these questions are addressed, several things should be considered. Choosing a theory is not difficult; almost everyone does it. But choosing the right one can be a problem. And that problem can be made easier by following certain guidelines. These involve identifying the initiating force at work, focusing on economic forces, and building upon the rich history of economic thought.

Many competing economic theories fail to identify the initiating cause. Among the most common are those that use interest rates or deficits to explain business cycles or growth. Both interest rates and deficits are the result or consequence of some initiating force. Recognizing this one crucial point permits us to discard many theories as, appropriately, voodoo.

Another aid in making the problem manageable is narrowing the focus of the initiating cause to the field of economics. To illustrate, it may be true that a rapid increase in the money supply is an initiating cause of a decline in the value of money. An equally important issue would be why those in charge of money increased it so rapidly. The answers to such questions involve a framework where issues may be dominated by factors outside the boundaries of economics. Greed, ignorance, or politics may play a role. Even if these factors represent the ultimate cause of a decline in the value of money, a theory dealing with these issues from an economic perspective can provide significant insights into the role of such non-economic factors.

Still another guide to choosing the appropriate theory is to recognize the rich history of economic thought. For over three hundred years, philosophers have pondered these issues. It is only reasonable to consider the explanations offered by those who have gone before.

These guidelines lead to adopting the following theories: for growth and prosperity, the main initiating forces are the degree of freedom in the market system and tax policy; for business cycles, the primary causal factor is a change in the money supply; and for the value of money, the focus is on all of the above.

Evidence and Observation

The confidence placed in any theory will depend not only on how reasonable it seems, but also on the evidence supporting the theory. What appears to be conclusive evidence can be highly subjective and can provide legitimate grounds for disagreement. If all of the above guidelines have been followed, the differences of opinion that remain should not be termed voodoo. Reasonable men and women can and do differ over what constitutes valid evidence. Some tend to be skeptics and insist on thorough support for any position. Others are convinced by the mere hint of a relationship between two factors. Usually, predetermined biases will have a lot to do with determining our initial position on the available evidence.

Whatever our conclusion regarding the evidence, it should be tentative. Conditions change. We change. As our sources of information become more complete, as we learn more about the world around us, we should be alert to how our new-found knowledge fits into the scheme of things. This awareness will enable us to reassess continually our confidence in those theories chosen, as well as our lack of confidence in those rejected.

Our structure for understanding how an economy operates is now complete. As mentioned, it centers on three major topics: growth and prosperity, business cycles and the value of money. Each of these must now be identified and analyzed separately. Once done, the interrelationship among these topics can be considered.

Chapter 5

Prosperity—
Identifying The Issue

O f all clues to the mysteries of economics, none is more sought after than the key to growth and prosperity. Having discovered the key and unlocked the door, policymakers can rest assured that generations yet unborn will reap the benefits of their discovery. To choose the wrong key, or to fail even to realize that the door exists, dooms future generations to a life of scarcity, poverty and despair. The history of economics tells of those who searched for the key and found it, those who searched but failed, and those who searched for the key to a different door.

The Nature of Growth and Prosperity

Before discussing the key to growth and prosperity it is important to understand clearly the objective. Prosperity means different things to different people at different times. Over 200 years ago the famous economist Adam Smith wrote that the living standard of the richest African prince did not approach that of the most lowly English subject. Today, the living standard of those Americans near the bottom rung of the economic ladder far exceeds that of the average worker in the Third World. What's even more impressive is that the average living standard in the U.S. has tended to double every thirty-five years. When growth is present, yesterday's prosperity becomes today's poverty. In this sense, prosperity cannot be viewed as a static condition; rather, it crackles with the dynamics of change. A stagnant economy, one that fails to

41

improve, will soon impoverish its citizens. The true meaning of wealth and prosperity is imbued with change—more today than yesterday, less today than tomorrow.

An excellent discussion of the nature of growth and prosperity is presented in George Gilder's influential book *Wealth and Poverty*. Gilder distinguishes the essence of wealth and poverty from various misconceptions. The perceived wealth of Saudi Arabia and Venezuela is contrasted to true wealth. True wealth is not embodied in the resources or assets owned or possessed by a country. Rather, it consists of the ability of people to improve their condition, to create more and better products with whatever resources are available.[1]

It is in this sense that the dynamics of growth and prosperity emerge—dynamics that make it meaningless to measure the state of poverty by looking at figures of how many people earn less than a certain income. A growing, prospering economy will always have a significant number of poor people. To the extent that this group includes a stream of people from other countries, attracted by the prospect of improving their lot, those listed as poor might be considered a testimonial to the economy's success. This is particularly true if, within a relatively short period of time (say a generation), the newly arrived immigrant can free himself and his family from the bonds of poverty.

For the U.S. economy, recent evidence testifies to the mobility of the poor. Researchers at the University of Michigan investigating the dynamics of poverty found that "between one-third and one-half of those who are poor in one year are not poor in the next." Moreover, only "2.6 percent of the population was persistently poor during the 1969-1978 period."[2]

The real essence of poverty is found amid those individuals and families who are unable to progress, those who continually fail to acquire the necessary skills or develop the appropriate incentives for improving their lot. Broad poverty statistics which fail to distinguish transient from endemic poverty are worse than useless. In the same vein, programs designed to reduce poverty by focusing on the consequences instead of the causes of endemic poverty are often counterproductive.

Regardless of the generosity of the gift, providing people with some of the fruits of prosperity without giving them appropriate insights into how those fruits are obtained, condemns them and their offspring to an ongoing state of poverty.

Dividends of Growth

Not all people place the same value on the economy's ability to produce material things. To some, growth and prosperity represent low-priority objectives. Before agreeing with that view, it is useful to consider some of the consequences of growth and prosperity. From the positive side, achieving the objective implies the elimination of absolute poverty and the opportunity for individuals to escape from a state of relative poverty. Comparisons over time between the living standards of people in successful economies and those in economies that have faltered show the true importance of growth. A wealthier economy can more easily afford to devote resources to clean up the environment, provide aid for the less fortunate members of society, enhance education, and provide for quality medical services and research.

In the United States, the wealthiest of all the nations of the world, over 10 percent of all income earned each year goes toward medical care to improve the length and quality of human life. In fact, so many resources have been devoted to prolonging life that even the moral leaders of society have questioned whether the extraordinary measures are worthwhile. Without a successful history of growth, an economy could not afford to support thousands of medical researchers whose sole function is to study disease and develop methods to relieve or eliminate the suffering and misery it brings throughout the world.

There are, of course, some ill effects of growth and prosperity. The enormous gap between those with the highest standard of living and those who are impoverished creates some difficult problems for both groups. The wealthy must deal with the issue of their moral obligation to those who have so little. And, those who are impoverished must deal not only with all the suffering that accompanies their lot, but also with the daily reminder that others prosper so extravagantly. Even so, balancing the good with the bad, few would consciously choose impoverishment. Without growth and prosperity, the dismal outlook of some of the early economists would have been correct. Disease, famine and war would have held the population in check. In spite of the problems associated with modern society, the alternative to growth offers scant solace. That alternative means that rather than being selective, poverty would exist everywhere.

Productivity—A Measure of Growth and Prosperity

As with so many concepts in economics, it is difficult to develop a precise measure for growth and prosperity. The concept of productivity is the best measure we have. Productivity refers to the output—goods or services—that can be produced with a certain amount of effort—such as an hour worked. The greater the productivity of an economy, the higher the living standards of its people. The faster productivity is *improving*, the greater the *improvement* in living standards. For most of the twentieth century productivity in the United States has increased an average of 2 percent per year. This has generally led to an improvement in living standards at much the same pace. While a 2 percent yearly rise in living standards may seem fairly modest, such performance leads to a doubling in living standards every thirty-five years!

An opportunity to enjoy the "good life" as most perceive it, and an even better life for one's children, depends critically on productivity performance. Those nations whose people are most productive are those whose policymakers have long since discovered and implemented the formula for growth and prosperity. Underdeveloped nations are not so fortunate. Their leaders failed either to find or implement such a formula. And, in some cases they failed to realize it even existed.

When the economies of the world are ranked in terms of their successful pursuit of achieving productivity and high living standards, the United States is at the top of the list. This will not always be true. Just as the United States replaced Great Britain as the most productive nation, it too will someday be replaced. Whether that day comes sooner or later will depend on the wisdom of today's leaders and their ability to recognize the keys to rising productivity.

Policymakers are constantly experimenting with the formula for growth. When they're successful, as Japan has been in recent decades, their productivity or efficiency can rise faster than that of the United States and they can begin to close the gap. The gap can be closed even more quickly if policymakers in the United States abandon the very elements that made the United States so successful. In the decade of the seventies, policymakers in many countries, including the United States, tinkered with the formula for growth. The result was a deteriorating trend in productivity, economic stagnation, and a frightening and unprecedented collapse in living standards. Policymakers were clearly losing the keys to prosperity.

Beginning in 1982, U.S. productivity once again began to improve. Unfortunately, tracking productivity performance can be tricky. Data on productivity provide only a rough guide to what is actually happening—as do all economic data. Furthermore, the data can temporarily swing up or down with booms and busts in the economy. When this occurs, it can obscure the underlying trend. And it is this underlying trend that depicts the basic health or lack of health in an economy. In this sense an economy with a strong productivity trend can be compared to a person in good health. Every now and then the person gets the flu and their physical condition temporarily deteriorates. But there is no long-term problem. An economy with a deteriorating productivity trend can be compared to a person suffering from cancer. They can still get the flu and recover from its symptoms, but the long-term prospects are discouraging.

The accompanying chart shows the behavior of one measure of productivity for the U.S. economy as well as estimates of the underlying trend (shown in brackets). Estimating the shifts in this underlying trend can be difficult and controversial. Those who want a handy guide to tracking productivity trends might look to the behavior of the stock market and to what is happening to the average worker's income after the effects of inflation have been removed. A surging stock market and rising living standards provide fairly good signals that a nation's underlying productivity trend is improving.

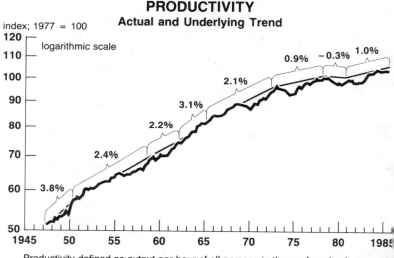

PRODUCTIVITY
Actual and Underlying Trend

index; 1977 = 100

logarithmic scale

Productivity defined as output per hour of all persons in the nonfarm business secto
Brackets show the underlying productivity trend as estimated by the Harris Banks'
Economic Research Office.
Source: Bureau of Labor Statistics; Harris Bank.

In recent years there has been an outpouring of excellent books and research studies, and even a modest change in policies, indicating some recognition of what went wrong with U.S. productivity in the seventies. Still, the preoccupation of so many policymakers, and even some economists, with the role of budget deficits, trade deficits, capital flows and interest rates strongly suggests that the secrets to growth and prosperity are once again in danger of remaining secrets.

And what are these secrets? What determines just how productive an economy is and whether it thrives or withers? Although some economists can provide a laundry list of factors, such lists usually confuse the characteristics of a productive economy with the initiating forces. The typical list includes such things as education and skills of the labor force, managerial expertise, investment in plant and equipment, expenditures on research, and so on. While these factors may be characteristic of a productive economy, using them to explain productivity performance evades the question.

Although education and managerial expertise are important, the motivation behind becoming more educated or more skilled is the essential factor. Similarly, investment in machines or research can be important for growth, but it is the reasons behind the investment that must be understood. To understand fully the behavior of productivity, it is important to focus on those key factors that initiate changes in incentives to invest and organize activity. Once the focus is placed on these initiating factors, the choice among alternative theories becomes easier. The factors chosen here consist of only two: the freedom in a nation's markets and its tax burden. And it is to these issues that we now turn.

Chapter 6

Explaining Prosperity
Free Market Theory

O ne of the greatest developments of all time is the free market system. This system, which can also be termed free enterprise or capitalism, involves placing a heavy reliance on the decisions of individuals to determine wages, prices, production and trade. The primary role of government under the free market system is to assure that the market system remains free of artificial barriers. Where regulation is deemed desirable, it may be imposed by government. However,such regulation should apply to all companies equally and should not interfere directly with wages, prices, production or trade.

The basic tenet of a free market system is that individuals who are free to make their own choices will provide the best solution to their basic economic problems. Sufficient food will be readily available, necessities provided, medical services supplied, houses built and investment for future needs assured. Not only will all these things get done, but if individuals are able to trade freely with other nations and choose their own political leaders, the end result will be the most efficient combination of resources for attaining growth and prosperity.

Historical Foundations

The nature of the free enterprise system is not a recent discovery. A number of philosophers began to unlock its secrets more than two hundred years ago. The greatest and most lasting insights in this area stem from the work of the famous

Scottish economist, Adam Smith. His book, *An Inquiry into the Nature and Causes of the Wealth of Nations*, which was first published in 1776, is one of a handful of economic books that have greatly influenced mankind. Smith presented a revolutionary new doctrine which emphasized the importance of the individual's decision and choice in economic progress. He argued that the greatest barrier to growth and prosperity was government interference. Artificial constraints either to assist or to restrain any industry would retard society's progress toward real wealth and greatness. Smith had the utmost respect for both individuals and their decisions. For in those decisions, the secret of the wealth of nations was to be found. From an economic perspective, the secret resides in free markets, and from a political perspective, it lies in the general liberty and security of the people.

Critics of the free enterprise system often argue that it is an unrealistic ideal, especially today. They point out that markets are never completely free and governments are frequently involved in aiding industries and their workers and in regulating the economy. It is important to recognize that the great defenders of free enterprise—Adam Smith, Friedrich Hayek, Milton Friedman—clearly recognized the important role to be played by government. They believed that government could and should regulate business and the environment; that government could and should assist the less fortunate in society; and, of course, that government should provide for defense and for so-called public goods that might not otherwise be produced. What the defenders of free enterprise also recognized was that the already formidable concentration of power in the hands of government could too easily lead to the type of restraints and subsidies that result in a crushing blow to productivity, wealth and freedom.

Explanation

There are two reasons why the free enterprise system is associated with maximizing growth and prosperity. The first deals with motivation and the second with information. While we enjoy doing things for others, most of us consider our own well-being and that of our families as our first priority. With free enterprise, more so than any other system, we tend to be affected directly by our choices. True, the nation as a whole would be worse off if we dozed off in school during a useful lecture, failed to work diligently to achieve success, or made a bad business or investment decision. However, the greatest loss is to ourselves and to those we love. In contrast, when we study, work hard and make wise decisions, not only do we add to the nation's well-being, we tend to obtain benefits for ourselves and those we care for most. Those of us making decisions that lead to the most efficient production of the items most desired by others tend to receive above-average income. Those whose decisions lead to a less efficient production of items, or to items that are not greatly desired by others, tend to receive below-average income. The dynamics of this arrangement, with its consequences for rewards and penalties, is what makes the system work. It motivates the largest number of individuals to strive continually for the most efficient use of a nation's resources in producing the items that individuals want most.

A second critical element in the success of free enterprise stems from the importance of the price system in providing information. The incredible complexity of all but the most primitive economy means that no one person can hope to understand all the factors that go into choosing the most efficient combination of resources to produce even the most trivial item. Fortunately, no one has to understand all the factors. So long as a system exists where the price of each item responds to market forces, the price of each item will contain all the information needed to maximize efficiency.

The real beauty of the price system is that it isn't necessary to know all the complex details of *why* the price of a certain item has changed: all we need to know is that it *has*. Shoppers respond daily to the information provided by the price system. When oranges become scarce and the price soars, consumers cut back their purchases. Only those with a great craving for oranges and lots of money continue to buy them at the higher price. Whether the scarcity of oranges results from infestation, a freeze in Florida, or some devious scheme of the Gay Liberation Movement, the result is the same—less oranges and higher prices. We may be curious about why the price of oranges has gone up, but whether we bother to learn the details or not, the change in price is reason enough for us to change our behavior.

A businessman who attempts to put together a product often has to make thousands of decisions. Among them are such issues as whether his product should contain more aluminum or copper or cardboard. Again, under a market system the price of the product contains all the economic information needed to make the most cost-efficient choice. It is not necessary to know that aluminum is in short supply because of an energy crisis, or that a new mining process has made copper more abundant, or that capacity constraints have led to a shortage of paper products. The price of the product contains all the relevant information on how badly others want each item as well as its availability. Armed with these insights, producers are able to assess the products in greatest demand as well as the most efficient combination of resources for producing them. Most important of all, the system is capable of responding quickly to change. The net impact of all changes affecting the supply or demand for any product is immediately captured in the market price. As prices change, this information enables individuals to make adjustments to ensure that production continues to reflect the most efficient combination of resources.[1]

For these reasons, the defenders of free enterprise believe that the system is a significant factor contributing to growth and prosperity. As such, economies characterized by such conditions should tend to be among the most efficient. When markets are free to adjust, living standards should tend to improve. In contrast, when markets are controlled by governments or monopolists, living standards should tend to suffer.

Evidence

One of the key difficulties in assessing the evidence surrounding free markets is the difficulty of measuring—or even identifying—the extent to which they exist. Adam Smith's evidence regarding the influence of free markets came from observing the world around him. He continually referred to the economic progress in England and to the favorable impact that free markets had on improving that progress. In addition, he was particularly fascinated with the development of the colonies. In their development he saw the evidence for his theories come to life. He noted that in many respects, Latin America appeared to offer greater promise for development. However, he felt its potential for progress was hindered by the lack of free markets.[2] In contrast, Smith viewed the freedom enjoyed by the English colonists as a key ingredient that would foster rapid growth and prosperity. Moreover, Smith made what must have been one of the most shocking (and accurate) predictions any economist has ever made. He suggested that the potential for growth in the English colonies was so great that their prosperity might one day exceed that of England herself.[3]

The first great economist not only extolled the virtues of free enterprise, but he attempted to show how it aided or hindered the growth and prosperity of various countries. Smith's theory regarding the benefits of free markets was put into practice in nineteenth-century England as well as in the United States. For much of the period that free markets dominated the economic policies of these countries, their progress in growth and prosperity made them the most dominant and influential countries in the world.

The theory of the role of freedom in promoting economic development and prosperity appears to have been validated by subsequent events. Where authoritarian rule and greater control over economic decisions prevailed, as in Latin America, economic progress was thwarted. Where free enterprise flourished, growth and prosperity followed in its wake.

Strange as it may seem, in the two hundred years since Adam Smith, economists have spent relatively little time and effort exploring the role of free enterprise in economic growth. Much of the present day theory of growth involves mathematical principles relating to the contribution of investment and labor. The role of free enterprise is often largely ignored. Moreover, the movement away from free markets in England (during most of the present century) and in the United States (during the decade of the seventies) suggests that even those countries whose development appears to owe the greatest debt to free markets do not appreciate them.

One of the problems in appreciating the contribution of free enterprise to economic growth is that economists have not succeeded in refining the measurement of freedom. In fact, when today's economists attempt to describe the importance of free markets, it becomes evident that the methodology has not changed in the past two hundred years.

Milton and Rose Friedman undertake such an attempt in their best selling book *Free to Choose*. The Friedmans attribute the golden age of Great Britain and the United States in the nineteenth century to a combination of economic and political freedom. They single out the role of freedom in agriculture, in which five percent of the U.S. workforce not only feeds the entire country but provides a surplus that makes the United States the largest single exporter of food in the world. In contrast, those economies that rely on "central direction by government—nations like Russia and its satellites, mainland China, Yugoslavia, and India employ from one-quarter to one-half of their workers in agriculture, yet frequently rely on U.S. agriculture to avoid mass starvation."[4]

According to the Friedmans the best contemporary example of free markets in action is Hong Kong.

A speck of land next to mainland China...with...14 times as many people per square mile as in Japan, 185 times as many in the United States. Yet they enjoy one of the highest standards of living in all of Asia—second only to Japan and perhaps Singapore.

Hong Kong has no tariffs or other restraints on international trade (except for a few "voluntary" restraints imposed by the United States and some other countries). It has no government direction of economic activity, no minimum wage laws, no fixing of prices. The resident's are free to buy from whom they want, to sell to whom they want, to invest however they want, to hire whom they want, to work for whom they want.[5]

The most important examples of limited government and free market societies according to the Friedmans are Great Britain from 1846 to the outbreak of World War I, the United States from its inception to the Great Depression, and Japan from 1867-1897. The example of Japan is important, according to the Friedmans, because its situation closely paralleled that of India in the thirty years following its independence in 1947. Whereas Japan during this period "relied primarily on voluntary cooperation and free markets—on the model of the Britain of its time, India relied on central economic planning—on the model of the Britain of its time."[6]

The contrast in outcomes between the two countries was dramatic. Whereas Japan grew so rapidly it was an international power by the end of the thirty year period, living standards in India remained virtually unchanged. The Friedmans attribute the differences in growth primarily to free versus controlled markets.

Other examples offered by the Friedmans of the contribution of free markets include the contrast between the development in East and West Germany following World War II, Russia and Yugoslavia (Yugoslavia having relatively more freedom), Israel and Egypt (Israel had the more vigorous market sector), and Malaysia, Singapore, Korea, Taiwan, Hong Kong and Japan (all thriving) versus India, Indonesia, and Communist China (characterized by central planning and economic stagnation).[7] Of course, the examples can change. More recently, Israel has come to rely more on government for the operation of its economy, while China and India have moved in the opposite direction.

It's fascinating that, over 200 years after Adam Smith wrote of the role of free markets in producing growth and prosperity, the Friedmans could reaffirm Smith's theories and provide a host of updated examples as evidence of their validity. But why then, 200 years after Adam Smith, would any political leaders ignore these theories and impose economic controls? It is not for want of articulate spokesmen that the case for free markets has floundered. Hayek, in his eloquent defense of freedom, argues that there is a systematic tendency for economic controls and the concentration of economic power to lead, not only to inefficiency and economic stagnation, but also to tyranny. Hitler's Germany, Mussolini's Italy, and Stalin's Russia serve as Hayek's empirical evidence.

Still, most economists ignore Smith, Hayek and the Friedmans. Most economists are busy attempting mathematically precise measurements of the role of capital and labor in promoting economic growth while ignoring the role of free markets. Why? Is it so obvious that free markets promote, while controls hamper growth and prosperity? To some economists it is. To Smith, Hayek and the Friedmans, the evidence is so persuasive and self-evident that it is difficult even to imagine a contrary view.

Is the evidence for the role of free markets self-apparent? Interestingly, it is not. The Friedmans, in supporting their view with "something very close to a controlled experiment" of the importance of free markets, contrast the Meiji Restoration in Japan, 1867 to 1897, to India in the thirty years following World War II. In addition to being eight decades apart, their example of a free market economy in Japan is clearly tainted.

> The Meiji government did intervene in many ways and played a key role in the process of development. It sent many Japanese abroad for technical training. It imported foreign experts. It established pilot plants in many industries and gave numerous subsidies to others....The state maintained a large interest only in shipbuilding and iron and steel industries that it thought necessary for military power. It maintained these industries because they were not attractive to private enterprise and required heavy government subsidies.[8]

The Friedmans considered the period of the Meiji Restoration as indicative of free markets because "at no time did ...[the government] try to control the total amount or direction of investment or the structure of output."[9] They argue that the "subsidies were a drain on Japanese resources. They impeded rather than stimulated Japanese economic progress."[10] But saying so does not make it so. If this is the closest economists can come to a "controlled experiment," then it is no wonder that the contribution of free markets to growth is still open to debate.

And what about Sweden, a country with one of the highest living standards, which has embraced socialism since the beginning of the 20th century? Interestingly, in spite of their avowed socialism and social welfare emphasis, Swedes pride themselves on free markets and a lack of government controls and, prior to the 1970s, low taxes. In fact, these characteristics led Hayek to characterize Great Britain in the 1970s as closer to the traditional concept of socialism, or a planned economy, than Sweden.[11] Are free markets more prevalent in Sweden or Great Britain? in Hong Kong or nineteenth-century England? in Japan or West Germany? Economists have not yet developed a framework for measuring, even in a highly imperfect form, the concept of a free market. Without measuring this concept, it is difficult to begin even to discuss the relative contribution of markets to growth and prosperity compared to the contribution of other factors.

In making their case for free markets, economists are forced to fall back on the same methodology that was used over 200 years ago—the imperfect, highly debatable procedure of referring in broad-brush fashion to the development of nations. By loosely characterizing some nations as free, others as more or less free, and concluding than whenever controls exist in a relatively free economy that they impede growth, is an approach that leaves much to be desired.

Smith, Hayek and the Friedmans have made significant contributions to our understanding the role of free enterprise. However, it is inexcusable that over the course of the past 200 years economists have ignored a more systematic approach to resolving the contribution of free markets to economic development. The development of a framework for measuring free markets is the first step in assessing their relative importance. Such a task would be extremely complex and time-consuming. But that is no reason for ignoring the project and turning resources to what might be the easier, but less substantive task of building models to gauge the contribution of investment or savings to growth.

For economists who might be interested in what could prove to be one of the most significant contributions of all time, a framework for measuring free markets in any country might begin by listing the key areas where freedom may or may not exist—international trade, the movement of wages and prices, the flow of resources. To begin with, can we measure the extent to which international trade in any economy is free? While it is impossible to do so perfectly, particularly when countries engage in export subsidies and "voluntary" import quotas, it should not be considered hopeless to develop an imperfect measure of the relative freedom of trade in different countries and at different points in time. The growth in imports and exports relative to the growth in the domestic economy can be a crude but effective proxy for measuring restraints on trade. And what of wages and prices? Can we measure at all the degree of freedom a company has in pricing a product, charging interest for funds or paying its workers? And finally, to what extent are labor and capital free to shift from one area to another? Are there significant government barriers to starting or ending any business, developing any products, raising capital? To what extent do government policies subsidize particular businesses or labor groups?

Even if all of the above could be quantified, there are questions regarding the interaction of free trade versus the free movement of wages and prices versus the free flow of labor and capital. Also, the relative importance of free trade to growth will differ depending upon the size of a country and the extent of its resources. In all, if economics is to advance as a science, a vast amount of work needs to be done to quantify the importance of free markets. Until such time, we must be content to rely on an established theory and a casual assessment of the evidence. The theory advises us that free markets represent the most efficient method of economic organization. The evidence, over a broad scope of historical experience, supports the view that free-enterprise economies tend to experience more rapid growth. Whether it's the development of the English colonies in North America versus the Spanish colonies in South America, West Germany versus East Germany, Hong Kong and Taiwain versus Mao's China, or Mao's China versus Xiaoping's China, the systematic pattern of development and growth under free markets appears to be well-documented.

Observation

It is, of course, necessary to continue to search for evidence regarding the impact of free markets. And new examples are always available. As the Chinese Communists, under the leadership of Deng Xiaoping, loosen government controls and permit greater freedom for individuals to produce and sell their produce, what is the impact on Chinese growth rates? Early indicators are nothing short of spectacular. In the five years from 1977-82 average income in China has doubled. A further monitoring of this phenomenon, as well as others, is necessary. Examples are continuously cropping up—the impact of private plots for agricultural production in Russia, where some 90 percent of output is produced on 10 percent of the land; the growth path in France after the widespread extension of controls by President Francios Mitterrand and the subsequent reversal; the development of the Carribbean nations following the removal of U.S. trade restrictions. As in so many areas, continued observation is necessary to gain further insights into the contribution of market forces in promoting growth and prosperity.

Chapter 7

Explaining Prosperity
Tax Theory

D eath and taxes, it is said, are among the few things in life we can take for granted. And appropriately enough, history is replete with complaints of individuals being taxed to death. Given the scope and influence of government, the power to tax is clearly the power to destroy—whether it concerns an individual, an industry, or a nation's effort to grow and prosper. It is interesting to note that a close relationship exists between taxes and the degree of freedom in markets. High tax rates can justifiably be viewed as an impediment to free markets. And any impediment to a free market can and has been referred to as a "tax" on that market. However, given the importance of government and its sources of revenue, it is useful to focus explicitly on tax policy as a second major key to growth and prosperity.

Historical Foundations

The view that taxes are a key factor influencing growth and prosperity has its roots in the writings of eighteenth century liberals. As with free markets, the importance of low taxes and their impact on incentives was one of the major themes of the *Wealth of Nations*. In it, Adam Smith argues that high tax rates can destroy the prospects for growth and result in the loss of government revenues. For Smith, the taxing of necessities was cruel and senseless. Also, he believed that a burdensome tax on business income or assets could easily be self-defeating, since it would simply persuade businessmen to locate elsewhere. Moreover, he argued that it is a mistake to think you can tax consumption in the belief that it is somehow better than taxing production, for "consumption is the sole end and purpose of all production. . ."[1]

In the United States, the Founding Fathers believed that moderate tax rates were so important to economic growth that they refused to give the federal government the power to tax income. And under the guidance they provided, the nation grew and prospered. Following in the tradition of Adam Smith, many of the great nineteenth-century economists reminded the public that taxes held the potential to stifle a nation's growth and prosperity. Of all those who wrote on the subject, none could match the flair and insights of Henry George. Writing a century ago, George provides a memorable picture of a scene as relevant to the 1980s as it was to the 1880s.

> ...to introduce a tariff bill into a congress or parliament is like throwing a banana into a cage of monkeys. No sooner is it proposed to protect one industry than all the industries that are capable of protection begin to screech and scramble for it. They are, in fact, forced to do so, for...every tax that raises prices for the encouragement of one industry must operate to discourage all other industries into which the products of that industry enter.[2]

Economic historians could search in vain for a more cogent, persuasive statement on the ill effects of taxation than that provided by George in his classic work, *Progress and Poverty.*

> The present method of taxation operates upon exchange like artificial deserts and mountains; it costs more to get goods through a custom house than it does to carry them around the world. It operates upon energy, and industry, and skill, and thrift, like a fine upon those qualities. If I have worked harder and built myself a good house while you have been contented to live in a hovel, the taxgatherer now comes annually to make me pay a penalty for my energy and industry, by taxing me more

than you. If I have saved while you wasted, I am mulct, while you are exempt. If a man build a ship we make him pay for his temerity, as though he had done injury to the state; if a railroad be opened, down comes the tax collector upon it, as though it were a public nuisance; if a manufactory be erected we levy upon it an annual sum which would go far toward making a handsome profit. We say we want capital, but if any one accumulate it, or bring it among us, we charge him for it as though we were giving him a privilege. We punish with a tax the man who covers barren fields with ripening grain, we fine him who puts up machinery, and him who drains a swamp....[3]

In spite of the eloquent warnings provided by economists, an understanding of the importance of tax policy to growth was gradually forgotten. By 1913, the Sixteenth Amendment to the Constitution was adopted, giving the federal government the power to tax income. And, it wasn't long before the inflation associated with World War I and its aftermath led to higher wages pushing people into higher tax brackets. However, taxes were reduced in the early twenties and President Coolidge was able to remind the public of some aspects of the nearly forgotten philosophy of the Founding Fathers.

I agree perfectly with those who wish to relieve the small taxpayer by getting the largest possible contribution from the people with large incomes. But if the rates on large incomes are so high that they disappear, the small taxpayers will be left to bear the entire burden. If, on the other hand, the rates are placed where they will get the most revenue from large incomes, then the small taxpayer will be relieved.[4]

Explanation

The central idea regarding the role of taxes is straightforward. If you tax something, you get less of it. By taxing productive effort without providing a service or product of equal value, government will tend to get less in the way of productive effort. Simple.

Although economists agree that at some point taxes become counterproductive, there is little agreement on where that point might be. Even more disturbing is the disagreement over which tax rates are most damaging to economic growth. Some economists emphasize average tax burdens based on the share of an economy's income devoted to government spending or taxes. Others emphasize the tax on buildings and machines as having a key impact on growth. Still others emphasize the importance of marginal tax rates—the tax rate that applies to any additional income. While any of these taxes may impact growth, there are reasons to suspect that the tax on additional income is the most important.

Identifying Tax Burdens

Measures of the average tax burden, based either on average tax receipts or on the share of income devoted to government programs, are too limited to adequately measure the burden on any economy. For example, government expenditures that transfer income to certain individuals could be replaced by a change in tax rates providing those individuals the same amount of money. The end result would be a major reduction in federal government spending and a comparable decrease in tax receipts, but no real change in the size of government aid. Furthermore, government programs differ significantly in the extent to which they impair growth. Those that help to build a much needed infrastructure have a positive impact on the economy, while those that discourage productive work by subsidizing leisure have a negative impact. Also, a rising share of income devoted to government could just as easily reflect a rundown economy as it could a runaway government.

Even with a relatively low share of income devoted to government, growth prospects easily can be destroyed when tax rates on additional income are prohibitive. India was typical of impoverished nations; for many years the government took more than half of all additional income before a worker reached the U.S. equivalent of $10,000.⁵ More recently, the government of India has opted for a major reduction in its tax rates. It apparently has recognized that when the worker is no longer the chief beneficiary of the fruits of his labor, the fruit tends to disappear. In the case of Tanzania, where the government took 95 percent of all income above $2,400, the entire tree disappeared! As a result of this type of problem, an average tax burden can provide a poor gauge for measuring the impact of taxes on growth.

Another measure of tax burdens—the tax on corporations—also has drawbacks. To begin with, corporations do not pay taxes any more than turkeys and houses pay taxes on turkeys and houses. From an economic standpoint a corporation is a piece of paper and there is no meaningful way you can tax a piece of paper. What corporations do is collect taxes. These tax payments come from people. They reflect some combination of lower returns to investors, lower wages to workers and higher prices to consumers. It is each of these respective groups that incur the true burden of the corporate tax. Precisely who bears the burden and how it may impact growth is a tricky issue. However, since corporate taxes represent a fairly small proportion of all taxes in the economy, their contribution to the overall tax burden may not be as critical as taxes that impact incomes more directly.

For the United States the best measure of the potential burden from taxes comes from the tax on additional income—the so-called marginal tax rate. This rate refers to the amount that must be paid to the government out of any additional income earned. For instance, Smedley, a worker at the local chemical plant, pays 20 percent of his $30,000 income in federal taxes. However, the government takes 40 percent of any additional income he earns. The 40 percent rate that applies to Smedley's additional income is his marginal tax rate. When Smedley decides whether to take a weekend job (more income) or work overtime (more income) or when Smedley's wife decides to work (more income), they must make the decision in light of the 40 percent marginal tax rate that applies to their additional income.

Since people produce solely for present or future consumption, incentives to produce depend on their ability to fulfill their wants. And this ability depends on the value of their after-tax income. Furthermore, it is the additions to after-tax income that are relevant when people make decisions on whether or not to engage in additional productive activities.

Impact of Marginal Tax Rates on Growth

Higher marginal tax rates hold the potential to damage growth in many ways. They can directly damage income and, along with it investment for the future, they also can result in an inefficient use of the economy's resources. Let's see how this comes about.

Since marginal tax rates apply to additional income, they can discourage such income from ever being produced. A rise in tax rates discourages certain groups from working at all. For low-income individuals the loss of welfare benefits that results from moving to higher income levels discourages legitimate, productive work. Likewise, when the wife or husband of a higher-income household finds that any additional income they earn is taxed at the highest rates, entry to the job market is discouraged. Also, higher tax rates can reduce the hours worked as individuals find an evening at home more attractive than overtime income. Resources are misallocated when an accountant finds it more attractive to paint his house in his spare time than to provide additional accounting services. This decision results from a compounding effect of higher taxes, which in the first instance causes any additional income earned by providing accounting services to be taxed at a higher rate, and second, causes the professional painter to demand a higher fee to compensate for his higher taxes. When accountants are painting their own houses, painters are fixing their own cars, and mechanics are doing their own accounting, resources are being misallocated and a nation's efficiency is hampered.

High marginal tax rates create additional problems when

individuals try to keep their additional income away from the government. By using tax shelters and deductions, individuals will shift resources toward those areas that provide the highest after-tax return to them. This will not necessarily involve the most productive use of these resources for the economy. The higher the marginal tax rate, the greater the incentive for redirecting resources. Also, the increase in demand for tax lawyers and accountants finds some of the nation's brightest minds helping to channel investment resources into areas that will lower tax burdens. These decisions direct resources away from their most productive uses and, hence, hamper economic efficiency. In addition, the positive contribution to growth of those talented individuals who become tax lawyers and accountants is not only lost but is perverted as their talents are unintentionally turned in the opposite direction. In effect, they become part of the cost of production instead of the fruits of production.

As tax rates rise, lower income individuals tend to work "off the books," or in what is now referred to as the underground economy. While the immediate economic benefits of this activity may exceed the costs, the difficulty or inability to advertise and expand, as well as the disdain for the law promoted by such activity, prevents the underground economy from being viewed as a positive factor.

No responsible economist doubts the potential for high tax rates to damage incentives to save and produce. The major disagreement among economists centers around the height to which tax rates must soar before these destructive tendencies become significant.

Evidence

Strange as it may seem, until recently, modern-day economists ignored the role of taxes in influencing growth and prosperity. Credit for waking up the entire profession goes to Professor Arthur Laffer who has popularized the view that tax burdens in many countries have become so great as to be counterproductive. Many economists were highly critical of this view, suggesting that it represented some new untried theory—perhaps even voodoo. Few realized that Laffer's views represent a critical part of the framework used by the Founding Fathers in drawing up the United States Constitution. Their objective was to design an economic system that would maximize individual freedom, growth and prosperity. In doing so, they clearly recognized the importance of moderate tax burdens.[6]

The first comprehensive attempt to relate taxes to growth and prosperity is found in Jude Wanniski's path-breaking book, *The Way the World Works*. Just as Adam Smith and the Friedmans provide broad observations from different economies to support their views on the importance of free markets, Wanniski provides a broad-brush approach to support the view that taxes have been a major factor impacting the wealth of nations.

And what a role they have played! Taxes, according to Wanniski, were a major factor in the rise and fall of the Roman empire, the American and French revolutions, the rise and fall of the British Empire, the rise and fall of Hitler, and the revival of the German and Japanese economies after World War II. As for the U.S. economy, Wanniski argues that tax policy was not only a key factor contributing to a change in living standards, but it has been the single most important factor leading to every business cycle since 1920. As if that weren't enough, high tax rates are viewed by Wanniski as "the essence of the Third-World problem of poverty."[7]

In each case, Wanniski documents the tax policy involved and its impact. The immense scope of his undertaking is sufficient to lead even the most skeptical observer to think twice before sanctioning higher taxes as a cure for anything. If taxes have done only a small fraction of the damage attributed to them by Wanniski, they would still represent a key element in the process of growth.

While the scope and breadth of Wanniski's book clearly make it the most significant economic book of the decade, his approach to evaluating the evidence of the impact of taxes on incentives and growth leaves much to be desired. Wanniski follows the approach used by Adam Smith and the Friedmans in their support of free markets. That is, without any systematic measure of either the tax burden or its changes, Wanniski goes from example to example through history to show how taxes affect growth. However, without a systematic procedure to quantify the impact of tax changes, it becomes difficult to show whether taxes or government interference with the market or some other force dominates the growth process.

This criticism does not negate Wanniski's accomplishments. Without a professional economist's training, Wanniski nevertheless exposes a critical area that had been almost entirely neglected by professional economists. These economists, it would appear, were so busy examining leaves that they completely missed the forest. Even so, casual empiricism as a methodology has its drawbacks. A failure to quantify accurately the tax burden that impedes growth and development, or the expected impact on incentives of a particular change in taxes, can produce more harm than good. It can lead to inadvertant increases in taxes or excessive optimism regarding fairly modest changes.

Measuring Marginal Tax Rates

Much of the empirical analysis of marginal tax rates has centered on the marginal rates as reported in the tax tables. As such, tax cuts are considered to have occurred whenever tax legislation is changed. There are several problems with this view. First, even the highest tax rates do very little damage if only a small amount of income is affected. A 100 percent individual tax rate on all income over a million dollars per day has little disincentive effect. Second, as inflation or real growth boosts income, individuals can move into higher tax brackets. Therefore, an effective increase in tax rates may occur even though official tax rates remain unchanged.

In 1981, the Economic Research Office at Chicago's Harris Bank completed a major study on tax rates.[8] The study avoids some of the pitfalls of earlier ones by focusing on what may be the most important tax rate for the U.S. economy—the effective marginal tax rate. This is the tax rate people actually pay on any additional income they earn. The particular households chosen were those in the 80th-85th percentile of all tax-payers. To be in the 80th percentile means that your income is higher than 80 percent of all households. This well-heeled group was chosen because of the relatively large amount of income concentrated around it. The idea is that changes in tax rates that affect large amounts of income can have a power-ful effect on activity. Incidently, for 1985 the adjusted gross income for a household in this group was approximately $40,000.

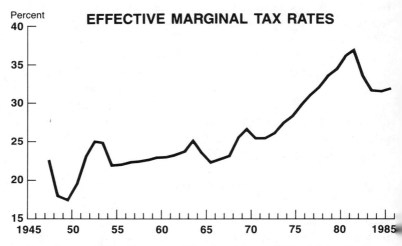

Tax rates on additional income paid by a married couple filing jointly with income in approximately the 80th to 85th percentile of tax returns.
Source: Harris Bank; National Bureau of Economic Research.

Throughout the decade of the 1960s a household in the 80th-85th percentile paid the federal government approxi-mately 25 percent on any additional income they earned. In the 1970s, as inflation pushed taxpayers into higher brackets and as tax loopholes were closed, the effective rates rose. By 1981 this same group was paying more than 35 percent of any additional income they earned to the federal government. The lower rates in 1982 and 1983 reflect the effects of legisla-tion reducing individuals' tax rates.

Tax Rates and Productivity Performance

The accompanying chart shows the changes in the underlying productivity trend for the U.S. economy that were discussed at the end of Chapter 5. It also shows what was happening to effective marginal tax rates when these changes were occurring. Since World War II, each time the underlying productivity trend changed, tax rates were changing in the opposite direction. These results suggest that tax changes have an extremely powerful effect on the underlying productivity trend. In fact, they strongly suggest that, for the U.S. economy, tax changes have been the dominant factor impacting underlying productivity changes during this period.[9]

Although recent studies on the relationship between tax rates and economic growth will be refined and extended in the future, the early results tend to confirm the wisdom of the Founding Fathers and of the eighteenth century liberal philosophers: The power to tax is truly the power to destroy.

CHANGES IN TAX RATES AND PRODUCTIVITY

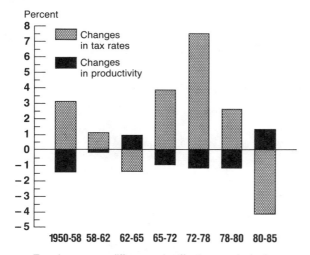

Tax changes are differences in effective marginal rates from beginning to end of period.
Productivity changes are differences in the annualized underlying trend from the previous period.
Source: Bureau of Labor Statistics; Harris Bank.

71

Chapter 8

Explaining Prosperity
Other Theories

M any economists reject the view that free markets and modest tax burdens represent the secrets to growth and prosperity. For them, the key to economic progress lies elsewhere. Some believe that a different key exists, while others are actively searching for a different door. This chapter will attempt to classify those who view economic progress in a different way.

Saving-Investment Theory

One of the most popular economic concepts contends that growth and prosperity result from saving and investment. To some extent, the concept is correct. For us as individuals, the more we save out of our current income, the more assets we may accumulate and the wealthier we may become. Similarly, when a nation saves for the future by shifting its spending from things that provide present enjoyment to the construction of buildings, machines, and other long-range improvements, there will be a greater tendency for more to be produced in the future. Even so, the saving-investment framework is not the formula for growth and prosperity.

It is not saving and investment as such, but the quality of the saving and investment that is critical. The Soviet Union directs close to one-third of its income to saving and investment, but its economy limps along—a model of inefficiency. In the United States, measures of the stock of capital (buildings and machines) show no increase between 1929 and 1950, yet productivity grew at an average rate of 2 percent per year during this period. Obviously, saving and investment may not always be related to economic growth. Massive saving and investment programs will not help an economy succeed if they result in projects that are not needed or that have been produced with an inefficient use of resources. Only in a free economy with moderate tax burdens is there a systematic tendency toward the most efficient and effective use of saving and investment to promote growth.

Big Government Theory

As a corollary to the saving-investment framework, some economists view government as the key to prosperity. They argue that individuals often tend to save less than is necessary for growth. As a result, they claim that government should force people to save more of their income through a high-tax policy. This theory views government as being able to take the people's income and apply it to projects that can promote growth. In this framework growth is largely a function of having the right investments: roads, dams, railroads, steelmills, and so on.

This theory assumes that because developed countries have a strong infrastructure and large capital intensive industries, these are essential to development. It also assumes that no matter how developed an economy, government officials and their advisors tend to be more capable of making decisions on growth-oriented expenditures than individuals in the private sector. The true foundations for this theory reside in an unshakable faith in the wisdom of the small number of people in government over the wisdom of the masses who comprise the market. In terms of support, all evidence that shows growth to be related to free markets and low tax rates automatically contradicts the big government theory.

Zero-Sum Theory

For some economists, economic growth is not the central issue. They tend to focus on the distribution of income within an economy. While this group will take growth and prosperity if it comes, it tends to be more concerned with the limitations on resources and with who gets what share of the pie.

The foundations for this school of thought are found in the writings of the Reverend Thomas Malthus and Karl Marx. Where Adam Smith was preoccupied with explaining how to achieve growth and prosperity, Malthus and Marx were preoccupied with other issues.

Malthus was concerned over the limits of resources, particularly food.

> ...*But as, by that law of our nature which makes food necessary to the life of man, population can never actually increase beyond the lowest nourishment capable to supporting it, a strong check on population, from the difficulty of acquiring food, must be constantly in operation.*[1]

He predicted continued misery for mankind, with starvation, wars and disease as the most likely checks on population. In Reverend Malthus' world, there is an urgent need to apply "moral restraint" to control the growth of population, and there exists a complex moral issue of how to distribute the limited resources among the population.

Marx was not preoccupied with how to attain growth and prosperity, but with the contribution of the laborer to the value of the final product. Note the difference between Adam Smith and Karl Marx as they present their views on the essential features of economics, or political economy, as it was referred to at the time. Smith wrote of "what is properly called Political Economy, or the nature and causes of the wealth of nations..."[2] While for Marx, the essence of economics revolved around what everything was worth. According to Marx "the pivot on which a clear comprehension of political economy turns" is the idea that labor possesses both a use value and an exchange value.[3]

To this day, much of the difference between economists and their analysis can be traced to whether they are preoccupied with growth and prosperity, as with Smith, or with the limits of resources or their value, as with Malthus and Marx.

The belief in the limits of resources, whether food or energy, stems from the Malthus-Marx school of thought. One of the most vocal present day followers of this school is Lester Thurow, Professor of Economics at Massachusetts Institute of Technology. The Malthus-Marx philosophy of the economics of scarcity and value is presented in the professors aptly titled book, *The Zero-Sum Society*, published in 1980. Several quotes from the book provide the flavor of an economist preoccupied, not with growth and prosperity, but with resource limitations and their distribution:

> *Politically, a declining economy means we have to be willing to make greater sacrifices in our personal consumption to maintain any level of world influence.*[4]

> *The American problem is not returning to some golden age of economic growth (there was no such golden age)...*[5]

> *This is the heart of our fundamental problem. Our economic problems are solvable. For most of our problems there are several solutions. But all these solutions have the characteristic that someone must suffer large economic losses.*[6]

> *...The problem is not in finding policies that would significantly accelerate economic growth (there are many), but in adopting policies that would inevitably cause significant income reductions for someone. To increase investment someone's share of the national product must decline.*[7]

Notice the key to productivity as seen by Thurow:

> *This means there are three factors that control the growth of productivity. First, how rapidly is the frontier of economic feasibility leading to higher-productivity activities. Second, how rapidly is the economy discarding low-productivity activities. And third, what is the distribution of activities between these extremes.*[8]

And by Marx:

> *The value of a commodity would therefore remain constant, if the labour time required for its production also remained constant. But the latter changes with every variation in the productiveness of labour. This productiveness is determined by various circumstances, amongst others, by the average amount of skill of the workmen, the state of science, and the degree of its practical application, the social organization of production, the extent and capabilities of the means of production, and by physical conditions.*[9]

While there is nothing incorrect in these last two statements, the framework used by this school of thought takes up the issue of productivity performance in mid-stream by assuming that it is largely independent of free markets and taxes. In their view, scientific innovation and efficiency will either occur or not occur, leaving an economy producing a given amount of output. In this framework, the central issue of economics focuses not upon growth promotion, but rather upon output distribution. Inevitably, this school goes on to conclude that the key role in economics is to direct resources to the individuals, groups, industries and areas where they "ought" to go. From there, it follows that the power to make such decisions—and to enforce them—can come from only one place: a centralized authority. In the search for the key to unlock the secrets to growth and prosperity, the zero sum group is clearly looking for a different door.

Chapter 9

Business Cycles
Identifying The Issue

While growth and prosperity are the most important issues facing any economy, they are not the ones that capture the daily headlines. Rather, cyclical developments—booms and busts—dominate the economic news. The euphoria brought about by roaring sales, new job prospects and higher profits has an immediate effect on our lifestyle. So do the despair and hardship accompanying a collapse in spending and the ensuing layoffs and bankruptcies. While the economy's development over a five- to ten-year period may be more important in the overall scheme of things, we must first experience the present. And if the present is going to be more or less painful, we ought to know about it.

As in the case of growth and prosperity, the first step in understanding the business cycle is to define what it is. Next, it's necessary to explain why cycles exist. Such an explanation involves selecting a theory that focuses on the dominant force that initiates cyclical swings. Once the theory is selected, surrounding evidence should be evaluated and alternative explanations reviewed. The final step, as before, is to observe events in light of the theory chosen.

What are Business Cycles?

Business cycles refer to the tendency of an economy to experience periods of rising business activity(recoveries) and periods of declining business activity (recessions). While the strength of recovery or the severity of a recession can be influenced by the economy's productivity trend, the nature of the business cycle involves a different focus. Growth and prosperity refer to the economy's underlying condition—whether it is fundamentally healthy or sick. In contrast, business cycles deal with an economy's temporary swings from booms to busts and back again. A recession or downturn in the business cycle can be compared with having the flu, while deteriorating productivity is akin to cancer. Still, business cycles are nothing to sneeze at. Although the odds are against it, the flu can be deadly.

Explaining Cycles With Voodoo

Many popular explanations of business cycles are not substantive. They either describe the characteristics of such cycles or they pick up the analysis in midstream by failing to identify an initiating cause. When these mistakes are made, the results can be categorized appropriately as voodoo.

Among the more popular descriptions of business cycles mistakenly viewed as explanations are: the consumer-oriented cycle, the investment cycle, and the inventory cycle. The following is typical of an interview with an economist who confuses an explanation of the cyclical process with its cause.

Moderator: *Could you please help us understand what happened to the economy last year?*

Economist: *Of course. To begin with, there was an explosive rise in business activity in the first half of the year, as consumers went on a rampage. Unfortunately, spending dried up in the second half and the economy weakened.*

Moderator: *But what caused this to occur?*

Economist: *Well, it's quite simple, really. In the first half consumers had enormous pent-up demands, business was rushing to meet those demands*

> *and inventories turned out to be unusually low. This meant that the manufacturers had to produce like crazy just to meet the demand. In the second half, consumers ran out of money, cut back their spending and inventories became so large that manufacturers had to cut back on production.*

Although the economist has described what occurred, the question was never really answered. Why do consumers behave as spendthrifts at certain times and as misers at others? While each society has its share of spendthrifts and misers, it would be strange indeed if every few years the spendthrifts turned into misers and then turned back again without any apparent reason. In fact, no such thing occurs.

While the openness of markets and the level of taxes will affect the proportion of misers and spendthrifts in any society, these factors will not turn misers to spendthrifts and spendthrifts back to misers every few years. For most people wants are insatiable. Except for a few poets and philosophers, people strive for more material goods and a better material existence. There has never been a scarcity of wants. With business cycles, the real issue to be resolved is why people can fulfill their wants more satisfactorily in some years (when the economy is booming) and less sufficiently in others (when a recession hits). Consumers and businessmen may become more euphoric over the prospects for economic expansion, but the key question is: Why the euphoria? A substantive answer must do more than describe the process. It must focus on the cause or, more precisely, on the systematic factor that initiates shifts in the public's spending patterns.

Some economists recognize the importance of searching for the initiating cause of business cycles and believe they have found it in either interest rates, budget deficits or trade deficits. Interest rates and deficits, however, cannot be viewed as initiating causes. To do so only leads to a type of circular reasoning that borders on voodoo. While the reason this is so will become more apparent after the chapters on interest rates and deficits, a few general observations are useful at this point.

Some observers argue that lower interest rates stimulate business activity while high rates stifle it. However, the interest rate does not simply appear out of thin air. There are many forces that cause interest rates to move in a particular direction. While some will directly stimulate business activity, others will not. Each factor can affect the economy differently. Hence, a failure to identify the sources of the interest rate change or the reason for high or low rates, can result in a complete misunderstanding of what is happening to both interest rates and to the economy.

A similar mistake is made when observers refer to a deficit as if it were an initiating cause. As with interest rates, deficits are the result of other factors. A deficit may change for many different reasons and each of these reasons can have a different effect on the economy.

To begin the analysis with a consequence—such as interest rates or deficits—instead of the cause can lead to a faulty analysis with damaging conclusions. It is much like punishing a failing student for his performance. There may be many reasons for the failure—laziness, a learning disability, a troubled mind or perhaps simple stupidity. Each of these reasons for poor grades tells us something very different about our student and each has different implications for dealing with the situation. A failure to recognize this point takes economic statements and analysis back to a primitive stage when incantations reigned supreme.

Not all explanations of the business cycle qualify as voodoo. We may legitimately disagree as to the cause of a student's poor grades. One observer may think the cause is a learning disability, another—laziness. By looking at the evidence—past grades, aptitude tests, interviews with the student—we hope to resolve the issue. Even so, the results of tests are open to interpretation and legitimate differences of opinion. At this juncture, careful observation becomes the ongoing way to resolve any remaining differences of opinion. And, this is the approach we shall use.

Chapter 10

Explaining Business Cycles
With Money

The monetarist theory views the money supply as the dominant factor contributing to the business cycle. If too much money enters the economy, it tends to produce a boom in spending. Too little money produces a bust. And just the right amount promotes spending at a steady pace.

Historical Foundations

Among the earliest explanations of the impact of money on business was that presented by the eighteenth-century philosopher David Hume. He argued that increases in money were beneficial to business activity, but only in the period immediately following the increase. Thereafter, an increase in money simply raised prices. Over the years, economists further refined their understanding of the process by which money impacts the economy. In 1802 Henry Thornton clearly spelled out the mechanism by which an increase in money impacts the economy. And in the early 1900s, in his famous text on money, Professor Ludwig von Mises of Vienna explained why increases in the supply of money led individuals to act in a way that would temporarily stimulate business activity.[1]

For almost 300 years economists had struggled to understand the impact of money on business activity. This investigation led to the view that a change "in the quantity of money introduces a dynamic factor into the static economic system."[2]

This factor sets into motion forces that lead individuals to act in such a way that economic activity is affected. When money is increased over and above the amount anticipated, there are pressures to stimulate spending. In contrast, when less money is produced than anticipated, it leads to pressures to slow the pace of spending. As a result of the rich history of economic thought, an important initiating cause of booms and busts has been clearly identified.

Explanation

While economists'explanations of the effect of money on business can be instructive, the essence of the process may be easier to understand by tracing the antics of Sam, the friendly neighborhood counterfeiter. Sam, operating in his basement, runs off $100 bills that look, feel and smell like the real thing! Being a fairly good-hearted person, Sam gives some of the money to his mother who lives down the street, some to his brother's family next door and the rest is spent at the local bar or placed with Sam's bookie. Although Sam has obviously contributed to the economy's money supply, he has not made a contribution to increasing real output. As a result, there are now additional claims to the economy's output without any comparable addition to output itself.

Sam's clan will use their money to place a claim to the economy's output. Since the suppliers have no way of knowing that Sam's clan's claims are not legitimate, resources will begin to be directed toward fulfilling such claims. Spending on final products will soar in Sam's neighborhood. The local merchants will find that business and profits are booming and they have to hire additional help to assure good service for their demanding patrons. The local bar buys a big screen T.V. and hires extra help to handle the crowd. And Sam's bookie has just rented a new luxury suite and installed a private phone to handle Sam's business as expeditiously as possible.

Unfortunately for Sam, just as the local boom gets rolling, the ever-alert Secret Service swoops down on Sam's scam. The jig is up. Sam is out of the money business and Sam's clan's supplemental income disappears. The local merchants can no longer support their added help. People are laid off. The mini-boom is over and in its wake is a mini-bust. Jobs, which for a brief time were readily available, are now gone. Sam's neighborhood has fallen on hard times—no matter that its income is back to where it was before Sam's venture. For the inhabitants of the neighborhood, its boom and bust—recovery and recession—were legitimate, even if their causes were not.

In essence, there are only two major differences between Sam's operation and the operation of a nation's central bank such as the Federal Reserve. One is legal, the other is economic. Since Sam is operating illegally, he has to work secretly in a basement, while the Fed operates in the open where all who choose can watch. Second, the Fed doesn't have a mother! Whereas Sam had to buy things for himself or give his money away to his mother in order to get it into the economy, the Fed has to operate in financial markets. Other than these differences, the economic effects in the wake of the Fed's operation are identical to those produced by Sam.

The Fed's impact in financial markets represents the major economic difference between the illegal activities of counterfeiters and the legal creation of money. In 1913, Congress voted to give the Fed the authority to write checks without having any money on hand. The Fed writes such checks when it buys Treasury bills or other government securities. When a bank presents these checks to the Fed for payment, the Fed simply informs the bank that the funds to cover the check are now available in the bank's account with the Fed. Presto! New funds have been added to the system.

When the Fed buys government securities in an effort to increase money, its purchases create a disturbance in financial markets. This disturbance leads to economic pressures that begin by increasing the demand for bonds and stocks and proceeds to increasing the demand for goods and services. Although the entire procedure is fairly complicated, here's a brief account of what happens.

When the Fed purchases government securities it bids up the price of those securities (otherwise no one would sell them to the Fed). This action tends to lower interest rates. In addition to raising the price of the securities, the Fed's action has further implications. To begin with, those who sold the securities to the Fed find themselves holding money instead of securities that pay interest. Second, all close substitutes to the securities that were sold become more attractive, since their prices are now lower relative to the securities bought by the Fed. As a result, those holding money have an overwhelming incentive to purchase the closest substitute to the securities they sold to the Fed. Nor does the action stop here. The next group that receives money for securities is in the same situation as the first. As they respond to overwhelming economic pressures, each group places upward pressure on the prices of financial assets—bonds, stocks and other close substitutes.

The process continues, and with each change of hands, a close substitute to the previously purchased item becomes more attractive. Since all assets (whether financial or real) have some close substitutes, every asset eventually will experience some increase in demand and some upward pressure on its price. As real assets (such as houses or autos) are affected, the pace of spending picks up. Demand for goods increases, just as it did in Sam's neighborhood, only now this demand has spread throughout the entire economy. Once the pace of spending picks up, so does the demand for credit to pay for producing the products now in demand. In order to satisfy these needs, more debt tends to be issued by those businesses that boost production. This increased demand for credit puts upward pressure on interest rates. Hence, the downward pressure on interest rates that accompanies the initial creation of money is soon offset by pressures that send interest rates higher. The rates themselves are merely responding to forces that stem from the money creation process.

Some economists have objected to the logic of this mechanism. They point out that as soon as people realize what's happening, financial markets will adjust completely to any change in money, thereby short-circuiting the entire process. There is an element of truth to this view. If 10 percent more money is created year after year, sooner or later the public and financial markets will completely adjust to that policy. Spending will bounce ahead at close to 10 percent each year. Unless the economy has an unusually high potential for growth in real output, inflation will occur. Interest rates will be high (but stable) in anticipation of both inflation and all the consequences of further 10 percent increases in money. Once an economy has fully adapted to a given increase in money, it takes a *change* in that increase to initiate a change in the established pattern of business activity.

For example, as people adjust all their decisions to an expected 10 percent increase in money, a major disturbance occurs if the money supply is not increased. In that case, all of the pressures noted above are reversed; the prices of financial assets come under downward pressure, interest rates initially move higher, and the pace of spending and business activity eventually slows.

Given that financial markets incorporate the expectations of individuals regarding spending and inflation, it takes an unexpected change in money to set the cyclical process in motion. However, given the difficulty in interpreting money numbers and the often erratic policies of the monetary authorities, most monetary policy developments can be viewed as unexpected.

Evidence

Today, almost all economists accept the view that money holds the potential to effect short-term swings in spending and business activity. This wasn't always the case. From the time of the Great Depression to the 1960s, the role of money was mostly ignored. Conventional wisdom had it that money played an insignificant role during the Depression and, therefore, it could not be very important in explaining business cycles. As is so often the case in economics, conventional "wisdom" wasn't very wise.

In the early 1960s Milton Friedman and Anna Schwartz published *A Monetary History of the United States*. In it they presented almost a century of evidence suggesting that changes in the nation's money supply had been a systematic factor explaining each recession and recovery for the previous century. Whenever the government created money at a more rapid rate, six to twelve months later spending tended to increase rapidly. When money was created at a slower rate, spending tended to slow. And when the amount of money in the economy actually fell, as it did in the early 1930s, spending dropped sharply, and the economy experienced its most severe recessions.

Could it be that the explanation for the business cycle was this simple? For the first time, economists had to cope with a new phenomenon: evidence. Strange as it may seem, generations of economists—despite a lack of evidence—had accepted the view that money was not very important in explaining business cycles. At first most economists scoffed at Friedman's view. They argued that the growth in money was merely a reflection of the public's demand for money. Of course this demand went down when business activity slowed and went up when booms occurred. Some argued that the public and even the banks, but not the government, controlled money. Others argued that the definition of money was so difficult to determine that it was impossible even to measure money, much less to use such an arbitrary measure to influence the economy.

As with all arguments in economics, each of these contains some elements of truth. Friedman and Schwartz had carefully considered each case in presenting their theory. It was the government, they said, that had primary control over money. From a technical standpoint, banks and the public can temporarily influence the amount of money in the economy, but their influence tends to be minimal and always can be swamped by the government's actions. After repeated denials, even officials at the Federal Reserve could be found admitting that, yes, they could control money. Today, few deny the government's potential to dominate the monetary process.

Is the change in money merely a reflection of the public's desire to hold money, or does it provide an independent influence on business activity? Friedman and Schwartz offer a number of examples of monetary policy moves that were clearly independent of business conditions. Furthermore, they show how, on all of these occasions, the economy danced to the tune of money—not the other way around.[3] Another charge—money is too difficult to define—has long been a favorite of money critics. It is revived in each cycle as observers conclude that, although the standard definitions of money may have worked well in the past, those definitions are no longer valid in a world that must surely have changed.

While it is never possible to establish a definitive measure of money—good for all places and all times—the enormous scope of the Friedman and Schwartz work is overwhelming. It suggests that while zeroing in on the precise measure of money in any instance can be important for refining the analysis, even without such attention there is often a strong relationship between money and spending.

The chart on the following page shows the historical relationship between spending and the behavior of money in the U.S. economy. It covers the period from the end of 1914, the year in which monthly data on the most common measure of money first appeared. The relationship is far from perfect. Clearly, factors other than money can and do influence spending. Shocks to the system such as wars or strikes, shifts in sentiment or psychology (independent of money), and any number of other factors do affect spending. However, the objective in explaining business cycles is not to describe each factor that may have an impact. The objective is to describe the major systematic force that initiates a change in spending.

While this first chart shows that annual changes in money have been closely related to changes in spending, it does not provide a clear indication of which came first. For this purpose a second chart is helpful.

The second chart focuses on the period since 1960. As does the previous one, it shows changes in money and changes in spending. But in this instance changes are plotted every *three* months. This extra detail shows that there has been a tendency for changes in money to *precede* those in spending. Both charts confirm the conclusions reached by the Friedman and Schwartz study:

MONEY AND TOTAL SPENDING

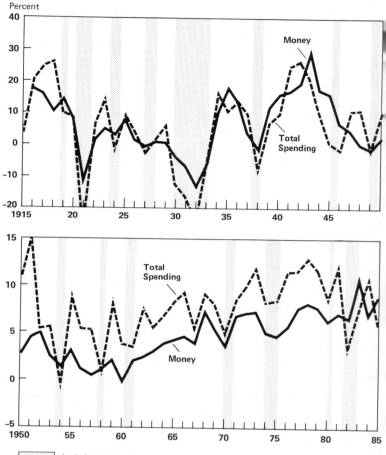

shaded areas represent recessions

Money data (M1) are defined as currency plus all checkable deposits at depository institutions. Total spending is defined as the gross national product.

All data are one-year rates of change, plotted annually.

Source: Federal Reserve Board; National Bureau of Economic Research; U.S. Department of Commerce.

Virtually every recession in this century was preceded by a significant slowdown in monetary growth; where the slowdown in money was greatest, the subsequent recessions have been the most severe; where the slowdown in money was brief, so were the ensuing recessions.

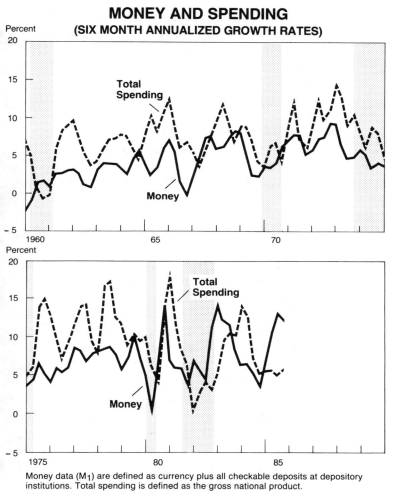

MONEY AND SPENDING
(SIX MONTH ANNUALIZED GROWTH RATES)

Money data (M₁) are defined as currency plus all checkable deposits at depository institutions. Total spending is defined as the gross national product.

All data are two-quarter annualized rates of change.

Source: Federal Reserve Board; U.S. Department of Commerce.

shaded areas represent recessions.

The most fascinating aspect of the entire Friedman-Schwartz contribution is that the dips and turns in money have been even more closely related to those in business activity since the early 1960s than during the historical period the two economists studied. One of the greatest mysteries in economics today may not be what causes the business cycle. Rather, the mystery may be why those who so readily accepted the unsubstantiated view that money is not a key factor have been so reluctant to accept the continually documented views that it is.

Observation

As with the choice of any other theory, evaluation of evidence regarding the monetarist view should be an ongoing process. In 1982-83 the evidence seemed to fail when the relationship between the growth in the money supply and the pace of spending appeared to undergo a major change. At the time, many who used money to analyze or forecast business cycles made some major mistakes. These mistakes called into question the validity of explaining cycles with money.

While doubts regarding the theory's legitimacy will continue, the particular problem in 1982-83 appeared to be related to measuring money. A major change in the powers of financial institutions occurred at this time. The change enabled banks to pay interest on checking account deposits, the main component of the M1 measure of money. Prior to 1982, banks were not permitted to pay interest on these deposits and, not surprisingly, the deposits increased less rapidly than other money assets. Once interest payments were permitted, checking account deposits temporarily grew much faster than other money assets and subsequently appeared to be growing more in line with those assets.

Changes in institutional factors surrounding money can and will affect specific numbers. A failure to recognize such developments will lead to faulty interpretations and bad predictions. Bad data notwithstanding, continued difficulties in interpreting the money data may mean that the theory itself should be replaced with a better one. A look at possible alternatives is next on the agenda.

Chapter 11

Explaining Business Cycles
Without Money

The view that money is the key to the business cycle has had a cycle all its own. Prior to World War II, this theory was widely accepted. After the war it was abandoned. Recently, it has been resurrected. The 1948 edition of the most popular college textbook on economics said this about money and business cycles: "Today, few economists regard Federal Reserve monetary policy as a panacea for controlling the business cycle...Only a minority of present-day economic experts hold out very high hopes for monetary policy to control a postwar boom." But in the 1985 edition the same author tells us that "money is the most powerful and useful tool that macroeconomic policy makers have at their disposal." And, "in the United States today, the central bank—our Federal Reserve System—is the most important factor in the making of macroeconomic policy."[1]

The author is telling us that after more than three and a half decades, he now believes that money has the potential to control the business cycle. However, he doesn't concede that money may be the main *cause* of those cycles. At this rate of revelation it could be the year 2022 before we encounter an edition of this book that attributes business cycles to money! For those who may not want to wait that long, it's useful to consider the validity of non-money explanations for the business cycle.

To begin with, it is helpful to understand that all non-money explanations for the business cycle are based on the assumption that people have the power and ability to change their spending independently of the amount of money in the economy. When Sam the counterfeiter spent his newly created money, there was an increase in spending throughout the economy. Sam's money was being spent along with that of everyone else. However, it is possible that in spite of Sam's contribution, spending would not increase throughout the entire economy. This could happen if the total amount of money (including Sam's) were to be exchanged at a slower rate. For example, if the amount of money in the economy (prior to Sam's intervention) were $1 billion, and the public produced and sold $5 billion worth of output each year, each dollar would have been exchanged for output an average of five times during the year. If before he was caught, Sam created and spent $1 million, and each of Sam's dollars were also exchanged five times a year, spending would have increased by $5 million over the course of a year. The only thing that could prevent such an increase would be if, for some reason, the public were to exchange its money at a slower rate. If the public were to begin exchanging money four times a year instead of five, then spending would actually drop sharply in spite of Sam's contribution.

All the non-money explanations of the business cycle assume that people systematically change the speed with which they exchange money. In this way, spending can be faster or slower than money alone would suggest. What specifically might cause this to happen is the basis for all the non-money explanations of the business cycle. These explanations have included such diverse factors as shocks to the system, swings in the public's mood or confidence, government spending, taxes, deficits, interest rates, and any of a host of other items that might appear powerful enough to cause the public to exchange its money at a different pace.

Historical Foundations

Most of the non-money explanations of the business cycle used today stem from the work of one man—the famous British economist John Maynard Keynes. His views, which were presented in the 1930s, changed the focus of more than two hundred years of economic thought. Where his predecessors believed that spending was inherently stable and not prone to fly off in one direction or another, Keynes believed the opposite. He saw the emotional instability of people as being the prime reason for business cycles. A loss of confidence, a gloomy outlook—these were the factors that caused people to exchange money more slowly, these were the factors that led to a slowdown in spending, these were the factors that caused recessions. Regaining confidence and optimism led people to exchange their money more rapidly, increase their spending, and produce an economic boom. Hence, Keynes traced the cause of the business cycle to "the uncontrollable and disobedient psychology of the business world."[2]

In Keynes' explanation of business cycles the public's mood became the dominant factor. Things would get worse, not necessarily because of any changes in policies or basic economic pressures, but because some gloomy force succeeded in altering the way people felt. This latter view created some interesting problems for economic forecasters. Harvard Professor Otto Eckstein, a well-respected forecaster, tells of the time he was roundly chastised by his colleagues for forecasting a recession. "They were afraid that the forecast itself would create such pessimism as to actually cause the recession," explained the Professor.

Keynes' predecessors believed that without an increase in money, more spending in one area of the economy could only occur if there were less spending in some other area. However, Keynes disagreed. He argued that the public's mood, not money, controlled its spending. As a result, any action that stimulated one part of the economy was now seen as lifting the spirits of anyone who came in contact with that sector. Keynes saw the condition of the economy as being similar to that of a delicately balanced scale. The slightest disturbance from any source was seen to be capable of hurling activity in one direction or another. Given this state, any shock—real or imagined—to the system was believed to be sufficient to cause spending to gallop ahead or come to a screeching halt.

Keynes concluded that government should take an active role in offsetting the emotional excesses of the private sector. He argued that when business activity was booming, government should temper the general euphoria by some combination of lower government spending, higher taxes and higher interest rates. If the public became depressed, government should pursue policies that raised its spirits. Here again, Keynes departed from the views of his predecessors. Whereas they had repeatedly warned of the potential destructive power of government, Keynes ignored such warnings and looked to the power of government as a force for stabilizing the economy.

In many ways Keynes' ideas were a startling change from the way economists traditionally had viewed the economic process. Nonetheless, his ideas permeated the profession and soon dominated conventional thought. To this day, in one form or another, they percolate through a vast majority of economic articles and statements. Was Keynes correct in setting aside several hundred years of economic thought? As time goes on, more people have become skeptical. And there are indications that Keynes himself was well aware of some of the problems with his theories. According to one of his contemporaries, Austrian economist Friedrich A. von Hayek, Keynes dominated economic opinion in a way that no single person ever had. "His main aim was always to influence current policy, and economic theory was for him simply a tool for this purpose."[3] Even more revealing is Hayek's intimate disclosure:

> *I can report from first-hand knowledge that, on the last occasion I discussed these matters with him, he was seriously alarmed by the agitation for credit expansion by some of his closest associates. He went so far as to assure me that if his theories, which had been badly needed in the deflation of the 1930s, should ever produce dangerous effects he would rapidly change public opinion in the right direction. A few weeks later he was dead and could not do it.*[4]

Whether or not Keynes intended his views to be used as a general description of how the economy works or of what causes business cycles is not important. What is important is that to this day, his beliefs are widely held. As a result, it is necessary to examine them carefully and determine the extent to which such views represent a valid alternative to money as an explanation of business cycles.

Explanation

One of the major differences between Keynes and his predecessors was the time period upon which they focused. Where his predecessors often viewed economic developments over an extended time period, Keynes' focus was on the immediate future. And the shorter the time period, the more control people have over the speed at which they exchange their money. In any one week, whether or not we decide to spend $100 on payday or keep it in our wallets until the end of the week is something we can control. Few would deny that in any particular month or two, spending can be faster or slower than what would be justified based on the amount of money in the system. However, for Keynes to be correct, people must be able to alter the rate at which they exchange their money for periods of longer than six months, for this is the relevant period of a business cycle.

According to Keynes, the initiating cause of the business cycle is a fickle public. When it becomes optimistic, it quickens the pace at which it exchanges its money and spending booms. When it becomes pessimistic, it slows the pace down. Even if people did have the power and ability to use money to suite their mood, such an explanation is not an economic rationale for business cycles. Blaming the cycles on the emotional swings of the populace begs the question. The substantive question is: What causes the emotional swings? Are they random phenomena, subject more to analysis by psychologists than by economists, or is there some systematic factor that tends to influence spending decisions? If a systematic factor exists, then the challenge of economics is to find this factor and learn as much about it as possible. If it does not exist, then using economic principles to analyze business cycles is a sham. If random shifts in the public's mood create booms and busts, then the principles of psychology, not economics, hold the key to explaining cycles. And if this is true, economists who believe it should become psychologists before attempting to discuss cycles. Until doing so, they should recognize they are making statements outside their field—statements that provide the grist from which voodoo can be easily distilled.

In the search for a systematic force that might lead people to change the rate at which they exchange money, there have been many suggestions. Some of these are more plausible than others. The most plausible are those that deal with shocks to the system such as a strike, war, embargo or earthquake. Any of these can—and have—led people to exchange their money faster or slower than usual. The most dramatic example of such a development occurred at the outbreak of the Korean War in 1950 when spending soared in spite of a fairly modest rise in the money supply. Fresh with memories of the many shortages in goods that were experienced during World War II, people spent money rapidly in an effort to hoard available items. While major shocks such as this do occur they are not a systematic factor that can explain most cycles.

Some have suggested that changes in tax rates may cause the public to exchange money at a faster or slower pace. And they may. Tax rates do qualify as a systematic economic force that may initiate a change in activity. In fact, in Chapter 7 taxes were viewed as a force initiating lasting changes in real economic activity. In the case of business cycles the argument is somewhat different. Here the focus is on transitory swings in spending rather than a more permanent creation of wealth. Some have suggested that a tax cut that stimulates real activity will also lead people to exchange their money at a faster pace so that spending increases faster than what might be justified based on money. This is an entirely reasonable theory. Whether it's also a good theory depends on the evidence.

In addition to changes in tax rates, alterations in government spending are often viewed as a force that can shift the pace at which the public exchanges its money. While a variation in government spending qualifies as a systematic economic force that may initiate a swing in activity, this explanation is not as plausible as the one associated with changes in tax rates.

While changes in tax rates may affect the amount of output produced, changes in government spending merely reallocate spending from one area to another. If the money supply is not altered and government spending is increased, then the only way to pay for the additional government spending is either to increase taxes or to borrow the money. In either of these cases the funds are no longer available to those whose taxes have gone up or to those who lent to the government. As a result, when government spending increases, private spending should be cut back. It seems odd to assume (as some economists do) that shifting spending toward the government and away from the private sector results in a tendency for people to exchange money at a faster rate and therefore increases spending, while shifting it back to the private sector (by slowing government spending) causes people to exchange money at a slower rate and therefore slows spending. What keeps this view from being classified as outright voodoo is not its questionable logic, but the fact that it does have a legitimate starting point—government spending—whose impact can be traced through the economy. While this is hardly a reason for accepting the view, it does fulfill the minimum requirement for beginning a legitimate analysis. As with a change in taxes, its validity depends on the evidence.

The real basis for the view that government spending affects the pace of total spending stems from the idea that the public mood affects its spending. In this regard government spending is supposed to raise the public's spirit. The reason for this can be traced ultimately to the belief that if the government had not spent the money, it would not have been spent. This view, however, is based on some confusion that often exists about the distinction between spending and saving. When a person decides not to spend part of his income and "puts it away for the future," the funds immediately become available to others. Banks and other savings institutions are in business to make sure that any funds that someone decides not to spend are quickly spent by someone else. Hence, the decision to spend or save does not represent a decision to use or not use the economy's output. In either case, the money is spent and someone uses the available output. Only if the money were buried in the ground would it not be spent. So the view that people control the business cycle through their decisions to spend or not spend rests on the implicit assumption that a large number of people systematically bury their money in the ground, thereby causing a recession. Then they systematically dig it up to produce a recovery. As noted above, even if this were an accurate description of how people react, it begs the question by not explaining why people might behave in such a strange manner.

When economists try to use principles of psychology to explain business cycles, their approach borders on voodoo. When they misuse principles of economics, they qualify as high priests in the primitive cult. This is the case when deficits, interest rates or the value of the dollar are used in an attempt to explain cycles. There is a fundamental flaw in using any of these factors to explain a change in spending. The error exists because all of these factors are consequences of other forces. They may move up or down in response to a whole host of forces, each of which may have widely different implications for the economy. Without identifying the forces that initiate a change in deficits or interest rates or in the value of the dollar, it is impossible to say anything meaningful about the effect they will have on spending. To do so is voodoo in the purest form.

Evidence and Observation

Can the public control how much spending it does by exchanging money at a faster or slower pace? To some extent, it can. The accompanying chart shows the *difference* between the change in spending and the change in money for each year since 1915. For example, if spending and money both changed at the same rate, such as ten percent, the difference between the two would be zero percentage points. In this case, the relationship between money and spending would be perfect. If spending were to rise by ten percent while money did not increase at all, the chart would show a difference of ten percentage points between spending and money.

In the years prior to 1950, it was not unusual for spending in any year to rise or fall by six percentage points more than the change in money alone would have suggested. Since 1950, however, spending has seldom been more than three percentage points from where money alone would have suggested.

The chart also shows that there is a systematic tendency for money to turn over more slowly during recessions and to turn over more rapidly during the early stages of a recovery. While this may be related to the public's confidence, the systematic nature of this response suggests that the change in mood is related to the change in the business climate. And this, in turn, is related to the change in money. The more dramatic the decline in money growth, the slower money changes hands. The more dramatic the increase in money, the faster money changes hands. This means that during recessions spending tends to be slower than might be expected—based on the behavior of money alone. During the initial stages of a recovery, however, spending tends to be faster.

Aside from this systematic tendency, the public appears to be able to exchange money at a more rapid rate in response to a shock to the system. The outbreak of the Korean War in 1950 is one such shock. At that time spending soared well above what would have been suggested by the behavior of money. While a major shock can directly affect the rate at which money is exchanged, such shocks have been few and far between.

The proposition that changes in tax rates can systematically lead people to exchange money at a faster or slower pace is not supported by evidence. Using either average tax rates or the series on marginal tax rates presented earlier, the conclusion is the same. Over the past thirty years there is no systematic tendency for money to be exchanged either more or less rapidly in response to a change in tax rates. While this suggests that changes in tax rates do not have an indepen-

SPENDING RELATIVE TO MONEY
Annual Rates of Change

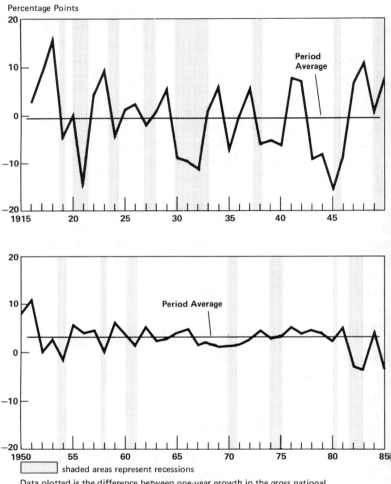

shaded areas represent recessions

Data plotted is the difference between one-year growth in the gross national product and one-year growth in the M1 measure of the money supply.

Period averages: 1916-1949 = −0.6%; 1950-85 = 3.2%

Source: Federal Reserve Board; National Bureau of Economic Research; U.S. Department of Commerce

dent affect on spending, it doesn't prove the case. In economics it is often impossible to prove anything. It can always be argued that some new, yet-to-be-discovered measure of tax rates will produce different results. However, for the time being there is no obvious support for the view that changes in tax rates have a major systematic effect on spending.

Similar results are found when changes in government spending are related to the rate at which money turns over. Over the past thirty years the rate at which money turns over has more often than not moved in the opposite direction to changes in government spending. Hence, there is no evidence to support the view that increases in government spending stimulate the economy by systematically leading to a faster exchange of money. As with the conclusion on tax rates, this one is only suggestive. It can always be argued that some new, as yet unknown measure of government spending will reverse these findings. But for now, there is no obvious support for the view that government spending, by itself, stimulates the economy.

So far, the evaluation of the evidence for Keynes' view of business cycles is fairly straightforward: No such evidence exists. Keynes did not provide any in his most influential book, *The General Theory of Employment, Interest and Money*. Nor has any emerged since. In fact, in the late 1960s, one economics professor at a leading university once went on at length, extolling the benefits of Keynes' theories. After he finished, he turned to the class and said, "It may be true that the monetarist school has all the evidence to support their view, but we Keynesians have the better theory." The lack of evidence appears to confirm Milton Friedman's assessment of Keynes' influence—"he shunted the car of economics on to a wrong line for some decades."[5]

At present, the available evidence suggests that the money supply is the key factor that influences spending in a predictable, systematic manner. If this is true, then the perceptions that characterize so much economic thinking must change. If money growth controls spending, attempts to save more income will not slow the pace of spending. Also, stimulating government spending or spending in any other sector of the economy does not lead everyone to feel better and thereby help the economy. It only improves the lot of those individuals directly affected. If total spending is governed by the growth in money, attempts to stimulate activity in one area of the economy will mean that resources will flow out of other areas and into those being stimulated. This is hardly a virtue unless one considers those areas being stimulated to be more desirable than those that are losing resources.

Finally, federal deficits lead to neither stimulus nor higher inflation, unless accompanied by faster money growth. And, if faster increases in the money supply do occur, then even the largest federal budget surpluses will not contain the rise in spending and the inflation that follows. While these positions appear to some as economic heresy, they are merely the logical conclusions to accepting the implications of more than two hundred years of economic inquiry, and rejecting the view that an emotionally unstable public is to blame for business cycles.

While the view that non-money factors explain business cycles has not been supported by any evidence, some may yet appear. As with other theories, observation is important. An innovative measure of tax rates or government spending or even new insights to consumer psychology may someday justify Keynes' analysis. Barring such a development, many of today's popular economic views that rest upon the foundations of Keynesian thought are destined to succumb to the regretable fate of the well-known dodo.

Chapter 12

The Value of Money
Identifying The Issue

Think of something you'd like to have—a new car, a house, a two-week cruise—anything at all. If you want it badly enough, the first thing you do is find out what it will cost. If you want a new car, and you happen to be an average worker living in the United States, the car may cost you $10,000, or half a year's pay. If you happen to be the average Japanese worker, you will have to pay almost 3 million yen for the same car. However, the 3 million yen is still less than a year's income. What makes a dollar worth so much and a yen so little? And why is $10,000 able to buy only one car today when fifty years ago the same amount of dollars could have bought twenty cars or a luxurious home? These are the issues surrounding the value of money. They are issues of great importance to a nation and to its individuals. Understanding the factors that determine the value of money is the first step toward determining what money will be worth in the future; and that, in turn, is an important step toward increasing your own wealth.

In assessing the value of money it would be ideal to focus on what determines the value of a house, a car, gold, stocks, bonds and any of the other things we might want to buy. Unfortunately, this task cannot be undertaken at this stage. One of the earliest and most difficult lessons regarding the value of money is that the factors determining the price of one specific product, such as a house or car, are completely different from those that determine the *average* level of prices in any economy. In fact, we could know everything there is to know about the supply and demand for every product except money and still have no idea of any product's price in terms of money. And we need to know only about the supply and demand for one item—money—to know all we need to about the average level of prices.

None of the above is obvious, so it may help to illustrate this point. Assume you found yourself on the planet Zoltar. And, through some strange power you were able to read the minds of all the inhabitants of that planet. You knew what products they wanted, how badly they wanted them, and, in addition, you knew the availability or lack of availability of all products. In fact, the only thing you are not aware of is the type of money that is used on this planet. With all your knowledge of specific items you would be able to tell people how much one item would be worth in terms of other items, but you couldn't tell how much they would be worth in terms of money. How could you since you don't even know what they use for money? Even if you were told that their money consisted of zolties instead of dollars you would not be any better off. You would need more information before you could determine what various items were worth in terms of zolties.

The information you would need consists of three things—1) the amount of money in the economy (in this case the amount of zolties), 2) how often the money is exchanged for goods and services, and 3) the amount of goods and services that can be produced over a certain period of time. These three pieces of information are all that is needed to determine the value of money in any economy. And changes in the value of money are the main reason that a house that sold for $10,000 in the 1940s might sell for $100,000 today. Before considering these changes, we must further discuss the elements contributing to the value of money: money, the frequency with which it is exchanged and real economic output.

Money

Money is both one of the most important and one of the most difficult topics in economics. Ever since they directed their attention toward its mysteries, economists have been baffled over this thing called money. Over three hundred years ago, English political economist Sir William Petty debated the ideal nature of money, the absurdity of increasing the money supply by proclaiming a lower gold content, and the view that a nation could have either too much or too little money.[1] In the centuries that followed, economists slowly and carefully unraveled the mysteries of this very complicated topic. By the beginning of the twentieth century the nature and importance of money was well understood. Money was viewed as a key element affecting business cycles and changes in the price level. Then along came the Great Depression. In its wake, conventional wisdom reversed three hundred years of progress in understanding the role of money. Money was no longer viewed as a key element affecting either the economy or the price level. In fact, by the middle of the twentieth century, money was relegated to the basement of economic thought.

More recently, the pendulum has swung to the other extreme. A former president of the Federal Reserve Bank of Minneapolis tells of a trip he made to northeastern Minnesota in 1981 to speak to a group of local union leaders. With the economy in disarray and interest rates at record levels, the Fed official braced for a hostile reception. "After I got through talking, there was a ominous silence," he says. Then, a tough-looking man in a corner of the room raised his hand: "Mr. Corrigan, I got a question for you. Why was M1 down $3 billion last week?"

Such close attention to money drives Fed officials up a wall. Mr. Corrigan concluded, "When you've got a miner on the iron range in Minnesota watching the weekly money supply numbers, I get a little bit worried about this country."[2] Since the Fed is primarily responsible for controlling the nation's money supply, its officials tend to worry whenever the public (or anyone else) scrutinizes their actions. Nonetheless, the miner from Minnesota apparently felt that the behavior of money had an important impact on his life. In this sense, he is closer to understanding the true nature of money than many government officials and economists whose monetary roots reach no further than the middle of the twentieth century.

With the de-emphasis of money that followed the Depression, many economists educated in the past three decades have studied neither the nature nor the mechanics of money. As a result, there is a great deal of confusion surrounding money and its related topics. Given the importance of this subject, it is essential to be aware of some of the key issues surrounding it.

What is Money?

Money consists of anything that is accepted in a given community as a common means of payment. It enables individuals to specialize in the production of a particular item with the full expectation that what they receive (money) for their product can be exchanged for any other item. Without money, it would be impossible for individuals to specialize in producing specific products. For this reason classical economists viewed the invention of money as second only to writing in laying the groundwork for the development of civilization. In all but the most primitive of societies, money will exist. Moreover, it will continue to exist so long as civilization lasts. The form that money takes will change from time to time and from community to community. In the age of computers, deposits in financial institutions may be transferred instantaneously from one person's account to another. Given the function that these balances perform, they are money. The precise form that money takes in any community will change at different times and in different places. However, the concept of money will not. Throughout history, money's role remains the same.

Where Money Comes From

The simple answer to the question of where money comes from can be given in one word: government. Today, in all major economies, government has the power and ability to create money. It decides what to call the money—whether it should be dollars, pounds, pesos or zolties. Moreover, there are no effective limits on the amount of money governments can create. In the United States, the government agency responsible for controlling money is the Federal Reserve. Understanding the essence of money involves recognizing the distinction between the Federal Reserve's role in the monetary process and that of all other economic agents. All legitimate economic agents, including individuals, businesses, banks and even the U.S. Treasury, must have money in the bank when they write a check for a purchase. Only the Federal Reserve and scofflaws continually write checks without having the funds in their accounts. Criminals are prosecuted, the Fed is not.

Most of the checks written by the Fed go toward purchasing government securities, such as Treasury bills, notes and bonds. Once the Fed writes its check to purchase these securities, the check gets deposited in a commercial bank that is a member of the Federal Reserve system. As a member of the Fed, this bank has an account with the Federal Reserve. When the check is presented to the Fed for payment, instead of debiting its account (as occurs with everyone else) the bookkeepers at the Fed merely credit the member bank's account for the amount of the check. Voila! Just like that, new money has been created. Accountants can rest assured knowing that the Fed's books balance since the liability to its member banks is offset by the government securities it purchased. Even so, any other legitimate checkwriter would have to have funds on hand in their account to clear their checks. The Fed does not. This is what makes the actions of the Fed so different from those of other legitimate economic agents. The ability to clear checks by simply telling a bank that the funds exist provides the potential for an unlimited source of money creation and that, in turn, represents a unique and powerful tool for influencing short-term changes in economic activity.

One interesting characteristic of a change in the money supply is that it comes closer to fulfilling the properties of a starting point than many other economic variables. Although banks and the public can influence the monetary claims in an economy, it is the Federal Reserve that reigns supreme.

Owing to its ability to buy or sell virtually unlimited amounts of securities, the actions of the Fed can easily dominate monetary developments. Much like Sam, the good-hearted counterfeiter in Chapter 10, the Fed can produce whatever amount of money it desires. Unlike Sam, it does not have to worry about the Secret Service closing down its operation. However, in determining how much money to create, the Fed must be attentive to the views of Congress, the administration and the public. Should a political consensus decide that the Fed's decisions on money were not in the best interests of the economy, the Fed too could suffer Sam's indignation.

What Money is Not

One of the most common mistakes in economics is to confuse money with credit. They are two totally different concepts. The nature of credit will be presented in the chapters on deficits and interest rates. At this point it's important to recognize that there is a difference between money and credit. Money is a common means of payment that can be created by governments. Credit results from shifting claims to real economic resources through time. Unlike money, credit cannot be *created* by governments.

Money Turnover

While the amount of money in any economy is important, equally important is how frequently the money is used or turned over. Going back to Zoltar, where money takes the form of zolties, we may be told that there are a billion zolties for use in the economy at any one time. How much a zolty is worth will depend not only on how many there are, but how often they are exchanged for useful products. If it took a week, on average, for a billion zolties to change hands, then over the course of a 52-week year, 52 billion zolties would have been spent.

The time it takes for money to go from one person to another in exchange for a final product will influence the value of money. If the 1 billion zolties changed hands twice each week, then total spending would amount to 104 billion zolties a year, but each zolty would only be worth half as much as it was in the previous instance. The reason for this is related to the final factor that influences the price level: real economic activity.

Money and Real Activity

The toil at work, the humming of machines, the transfer of goods and services...These are the nuts and bolts of any economy. In order for any productive activity to occur, the economy's resources—its labor, machines and raw materials —must be brought together to produce useful products. These resources are often referred to as real resources and the final output produced is, naturally, real output. The use of resources has a time dimension associated with it. It doesn't make any sense to ask how much an economy can produce with its resources until we determine the time period involved. For a certain time period, such as a year, the issue of how much real output can be produced becomes a meaningful issue. The amount of output will depend in large part on the nature of an economy's resources. If, as a result of many years of investment and research, an economy has a large amount of advanced machinery, buildings, skilled labor, and developed land, then its accumulated resources will enable it to produce far more in any given year than an economy without such an accumulation.

If it were not for money, understanding economics would be much easier. The value of any item could simply be expressed in terms of other items or in terms of an hour worked by the average worker. A car might be exchanged for a small piece of undeveloped land or for six months of work performed by the average worker. In such an economy, no one would have to worry about the price level. However, without money, the economy would become so bogged down by people searching for a match between what they had to offer and what they wanted that not much of anything would be produced.

It is in its role as a common means of payment that money relates to real activity. Money represents the means whereby individuals can direct the use of the economy's resources to fulfill their desires. Anyone who makes a decision to spend money sends signals to shift the use of the economy's resources toward the area affected and away from other areas. A decision to build a home instead of taking a vacation shifts resources away from tourism, airline and hotel-related items directing them instead toward earth-moving equipment, cement, lumber and other construction-oriented activities. In this sense, those who have money hold sway over the use of the economy's resources. While the resources that produce output are the main ingredients in any economy, money plays a major role in efficiently directing the use of those resources.

The Value of Money

Money, how often it is exchanged and the amount of goods and services produced—all these combine to determine money's value at any particular time. On the planet Zoltar (or anywhere else) we can determine what money is worth with this information. The 52 billion zolties that are spent each year are equal to all the goods and services produced on Zoltar that year. Hence, the total amount of goods and services is valued at 52 billion zolties. The value of money or the average level of prices simply tell us what the goods and services are worth at that point in time. If Zoltar had twice as many zolties or if the average zolty were exchanged twice a week and the annual output of goods and services were the same as before, Zoltar's economy would be no better off than before even though prices would be twice as high and its money worth half as much.

The average level of prices for any economy is simply a point of reference for valuing the output of that economy in terms of its money. It is not very useful to know that Zoltar's economy produces a 104 billion zolties worth of goods in a year, while the United States produces 4 trillion dollars worth of output. Until we know what a zolty or a dollar or a yen will buy we cannot determine the value of any of this money. In order to determine the value of money we have to relate it to the products it can buy. This is true for any country's money. If 10,000 U.S. dollars buys a standard car, then this is what $10,000 is worth. If it takes 3 million yen to buy the same car, then $10,000 is worth the equivalent of 3 million yen, or $1 is worth 300 yen. If the car sells for 500 zolties on Zoltar (let's set aside shipping and other such costs), then $10,000 is equivalent to 500 zolties,or $1 = .05 zolties. What a currency is worth in terms of another currency depends primarily on what it will buy.

Changes in the Value of Money

Once the value of money has been determined, its value can change. This is where the concept of a price level comes in handy. As the price level changes it shows a change in the value of money (what the money will buy). Going back to Zoltar we can show that the price level can change for any one of three reasons—the amount of money (zolties) changes, the speed at which zolties are exchanged for output changes, or the amount of the output changes.

If the amount of zolties or the speed at which they are exchanged for output doubles, the price level on Zoltar also doubles. Prices would also double if the amount of output produced were cut in half while spending remained the same. Since 52 billion zolties would be spent to purchase only half the output it used to buy, the value of the zolty would be half what is was and prices would be twice what they were.

Returning to earth, we can apply the same principles to understand why the price level for any country might change. It might change due to an increase in that country's money (regardless of what the money is called), or to a variation in the speed that money is exchanged for goods and services or to a shift in real output. Isolating which of these factors is the dominant one, or the one most important in determining changes in the value of money, involves choosing a theory or explanation of why the value of money changes. Hence, our next topic.

Chapter 13

Changes in the Value of Money
Choosing a Theory

I dentifying the factors that can lead to changes in the value of money is the first step in explaining why such changes come about. The second step is choosing a theory or explanation for those changes. The theory should identify the primary initiating economic force that tends to produce changes in the value of money. Is this force the money supply, the speed at which money turns over, or real output?

Throughout history, the usual change in the value of money has been in one direction: down. Money becomes less valuable when the general price level is increasing. And an ongoing increase in an economy's price level is known as inflation. An ongoing decline in the general price level is deflation. It has been over fifty years since the U.S. economy experienced deflation. As a result, the focus of our discussion regarding a change in the price level tends to be on inflation. It begins with a survey of the traditional explanation of inflation: too much money.

Monetary Theory

Discussions on the nature and effects of inflation are not new. Their origins extend at least as far back as the 14th century.[1] By the sixteenth-century, the French monetary analyst, Jean Bodin, argued that the "main and almost sole" cause of rising prices was "the abundance of gold and silver."[2] Others who pondered the nature of money at this time came to recognize the distinction between the prices of each individual item and those of all items.[3] They recognized that an increase in the price of one item, or even several critical items such as food, clothing and oil, does not constitute inflation. In a dynamic economy prices are always changing. Some rise and others fall. In fact, such movements in specific prices provide crucial information about the availability of resources—information that is essential to the efficient operation of any economy.

By the middle of the eighteenth century, economists believed that the essence of inflation was the result of an increase in a nation's money supply.[4] Henry Thornton in 1802 presented the idea that paper money was governed by the same laws of supply and demand as other commodities, and that the speed at which money changed hands could also have an effect on inflation.[5] By the beginning of the twentieth century, economic opinion had settled on a change in the supply of money as being the primary explanation for inflation, while recognizing that the speed at which money turns over can sometimes play a secondary role.[6] Hence, for more than two centuries, money supply had been viewed as the key force determining inflation.

Explanation

To help understand the mechanism by which money creates inflation, imagine that our counterfeiter, Sam, who set up shop in Chapter 10, is not caught. As he increases the supply of money there is greater and greater spending throughout his neighborhood. Those who exchanged goods and services for the bogus bills have no way of knowing what is happening. They are fooled into exchanging their services for dollars that will soon purchase less than they expected. Still, at the time, they do not know that more money is being put into the system, nor that its value must fall.

Eventually, spending booms beyond Sam's neighborhood. Since nothing has happened to increase the economy's resources, individuals will find that progressively greater amounts of money must be offered to control the limited amount of output available. In the process, prices are bid up.

The more money that is created, the greater the pressure on prices.

Evidence

The view that money is the key initiating factor contributing to inflation has a long history in economic thought. It is entirely reasonable to suspect that the creation of more money will cause it to be worth less. What remains is observation. To what extent have increases in money been associated with changes in inflation?

In reviewing the evidence on money and inflation it is important to keep certain things in mind. To begin with, the economic concepts of money and inflation have to be measured. Measuring economic concepts can be difficult. The accompanying chart shows how different measures of inflation have behaved for the past seventy years. Although the general patterns are often the same, there can be noticeable disparities between different series, all of which attempt to measure a change in prices. The same holds true for money. A judgment has to be made as to which specific measures of money and inflation are closest to the economic concepts. Regardless of the choice, there are times when a particular measure of inflation or a particular measure of money may be misleading. When price controls are placed on an economy (as occurred during World War II, the Korean War and the early 1970s), measures of inflation become distorted. Likewise, when there is a major institutional change in the financial system (as occurred in the early 1980s), money numbers can become distorted.

In spite of all these caveats, the second chart confirms that a relationship between changes in money and changes in inflation does exist. Since economic data are erratic from month to month, the inflation numbers are averaged over an entire year. And, since there is usually a lag of two to three years between a change in money and a change in inflation, the money data are averaged over a three-year period. Some of the largest discrepancies, such as those of the mid-1940s, 1950 and the early 1970s, were characterized by the outbreak of war or price controls. And, in the early 1980s the measurement of money was affected by changes in regulations. (See page 92.) These exceptions, as well as others, suggest that factors other than money can influence inflation. However, over time, changes in the supply of money appear to be the

MEASURES OF INFLATION

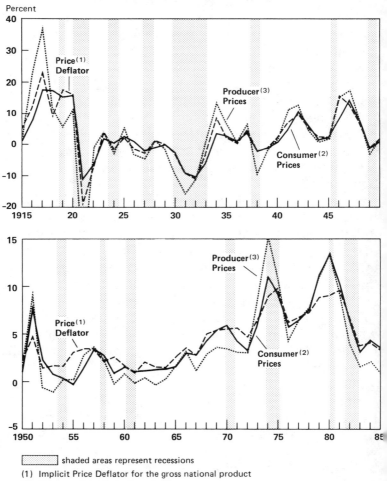

shaded areas represent recessions

(1) Implicit Price Deflator for the gross national product
(2) Consumer Price Index for urban consumers
(3) Producer Price Index
All data are one-year rates of change, plotted annually.
Source: U.S. Department of Commerce; U.S. Department of Labor.

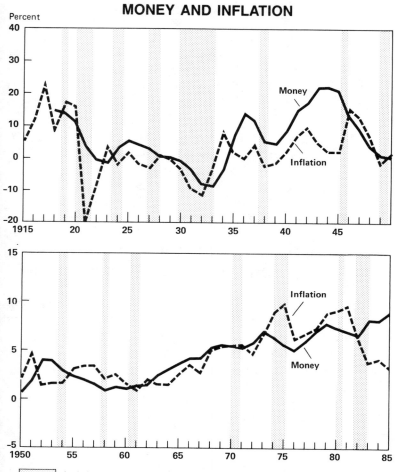

MONEY AND INFLATION

shaded areas represent recessions

Money data (M1) are defined as currency plus all checkable deposits at depository institutions. The data are 3 year annualized rates of change, plotted annually.

Inflation is measured by the implicit price deflator for the gross national product. The data are one-year rates of change, plotted annually.

Source: Federal Reserve Board; National Bureau of Economic Research; U.S. Department of Commerce.

dominant factor that has long been associated with a change in its value.

The two alternatives to the view that money is the key factor in explaining inflation focus either on the speed at which money changes hands or on real output. Each of these will be examined in turn.

119

Money Turnover Theory

Although this theory has emerged several times in each of the past four centuries, its most recent appearance can be credited to John Maynard Keynes. Just as Keynes altered so many views on the nature of business cycles, he also changed views with respect to inflation. Under Keynes' theory, the same factors that might affect the speed at which money exchanged hands to cause a change in spending were also seen as holding the potential to affect the value of money. Remember, Keynes believed that changes in psychology and sentiment were strong enough to cause cycles of booms and busts in the economy. If individuals held such enormous power, it only followed that they should also be able to raise prices whenever the spirit moved them.

In focusing on the causes of inflation Keynes emphasized the importance of wages and the ability of workers to control them. This emphasis on the role of wages in determining prices set economists off in a myriad of directions in explaining inflation. While the classical economists had viewed a wage as just another price—the price of labor—the idea that wages could represent a unique factor in explaining inflation was readily accepted by Keynes' followers. Since we are all laborers, it is nice to think of the price of our services as somehow unique from those of all the various non-human commodities. To quote Keynes:

> "...The long-run stability or instability of prices will depend on the strength of the upward trend of the wage unit (or, more precisely, of the cost unit) compared with the rate of increase in the efficiency of the productive system."[7]

The view that wages were a unique, independent factor contributing to inflation had great appeal. After all, didn't wages and salaries account for 80 percent of the value of all products? Moreover, almost every businessman knew that when his labor cost rose, he was forced to raise the price of his product. What could be more obvious than the view that inflation was caused by an increase in wages? Nothing could be more obvious, nor as it turns out, more wrong.

The idea of focusing on the power of the workers to demand higher and higher wages was followed by other fascinating explanations of inflation. If one particular price—that of labor—could cause a rise in the overall price level, why couldn't other prices have the same effect? Why couldn't higher food prices or higher energy prices or higher housing costs all lead to higher inflation?

The culmination of the view that higher costs led to inflation probably occurred when President Carter's economists blamed the rapid inflation of the late 1970s on higher prices for food, energy, housing and medical services. If it weren't for these items, they argued, the inflation rate wouldn't be all that bad. These economists were weaned on what was called the cost-push theory of inflation—the view that the cost of particular items determined their prices.

> As an abrupt increase in the price of an important commodity translates into an increase in the cost of living, pressure builds for wage gains to match the new inflation. Some gains take place automatically where wages are linked to prices through cost-of-living clauses in union contracts. Additional acceleration occurs as new contracts are negotiated. As businesses observe the rising wage-price spiral, they are likely to expect a higher future level of inflation. They are then somewhat more likely to grant larger wage increases, both in the belief that rising inflation will make it possible to pass through increases in higher prices and in order to avoid losing workers. Through this process, a sharp increase in food or oil prices can lead to a rise in the underlying inflation rate.[8]

What's wrong with the view that higher costs for labor, energy, shelter, food, etc., cause higher prices? First, a cost to one group is a price to another. To businessmen, wages are a cost; but to workers, that same wage is the price of their services. To the consumer, maintaining a household depends critically on the cost of food. However, to farmers, it is the price of the food that determines their income. The amount spent on each item, which appears as a cost to the group that is paying for it, is a price to the group receiving payment. As a result, the cost-push theory of inflation can just as easily be termed the price-push theory—prices go up because prices go up (not a very substantive explanation).

In essence, the cost-push view of inflation went hand in hand with the view that shifts in sentiment caused business cycles. It assumed that the decisions of private individuals, which held the potential to send the economy into a boom or bust, also held the potential to raise wages or prices in such a manner as to usher in an inflationary period.

The mechanism by which this was accomplished was through the speed at which money was turned over. It was believed that individuals would respond to shocks to the system—such as a rise in the price of oil—by turning money over more rapidly so as to pay for the higher-priced oil as well as all their other purchases. In other words, individuals were believed to be capable of systematically adjusting the speed at which they turned over their money, not just to control business cycles, but to control inflation as well.

Do individuals have the power and ability to adjust their use of money to changing circumstances? While the classical economists said no, Keynes and his followers said yes. Evidence and observation can help to resolve the conflict.

Evidence and Observation

If consumers, workers or natural shocks to the system provided the initiating force for an inflationary cycle, then prices should begin to rise before or at least coincide with an increase in money. If price increases tend to follow increases in money creation, it should be clear that the monetary authorities are initiating the inflationary process, and not reacting to it in self defense. The chart in the previous chapter strongly suggests that inflation has tended to follow broad movements in money. It is not the other way around. Furthermore, the lack of success in the 1970s in dealing with U.S.

inflation under wage and price guidelines and controls should be compared to the success encountered in the early 1980s, when monetary restraint was applied. This example is only the most recent of many observations suggesting that the classical economists were on the right track in believing that the money supply was the key force explaining inflation.

Real Growth Theory

The final view of inflation considers the performance of the economy as the dominant force in the process. Do changes in an economy's ability to produce output represent the key to the inflationary process? Perhaps. Such changes have both a direct and indirect effect on the value of money. The direct effect results from the link between the amount of real output produced and the value of money. If an economy's policies are geared toward producing more real output with the same amount of spending, money would be worth more than it would be if less output were produced. However, shifts in an economy's ability to produce output tend to be fairly modest. A shift of 2 percent per year often means the difference between a healthy, prospering economy and one that is fundamentally sick. As a result, the direct effect on the value of money from economic performance is relatively small— seldom amounting to more than 2 percent in any year.

However, the performance of the economy may have an important indirect effect on the value of money. If people are prospering and real incomes are rising, there is little political pressure on the monetary authorities to create too much money. As a result, responsible behavior may prevail and inflation may be more likely to be contained. In contrast, if people are disappointed with the economy's performance, they are more likely to pressure the monetary authorities into creating more money to improve their situation. In fact, this indirect phenomenon appears to have played an important role in both the inflationary spiral of the 1970s and its reversal in the early 1980s.

Since increases in real output mean that more spending goes for real growth and less for inflation, there should be

123

less political pressure on the monetary authorities when growth is strong. Whether or not real growth is the primary factor in the inflation process is subject to testing. The instances of strong growth accompanied by high inflation tend to reduce confidence in the theory that economic performance is the dominant force in the inflationary process.

The idea that economic performance might influence the behavior of the monetary authorities raises some interesting questions about why those authorities behave as they do. In addition to economic performance, there are at least two other reasons to suggest why governments create too much money. One is that such behavior stems from ignorance; the monetary authorities are simply not smart enough to know how much money to produce to attain price stability, so they fail to attain it. A second is that the money authorities know exactly what they are doing and that the main purpose of inflationary cycles is to redistribute income.

What is the true starting point for inflation? In all likelihood, all three of the arguments listed above have some degree of truth to them. Those who control the money process at different times will have a different depth of understanding. Hence, ignorance or knowledge can play a part. Also, the desire to redistribute income may lead to conscious or unconscious decisions to inflate or deflate. And, the ability to carry through any policy will be affected by economic conditions. Few want to rock the boat while prosperity abounds. While the true starting point in the inflationary process is debatable, the debate should begin with an understanding of money and its role in the inflationary process. From there, the potential interaction between inflation and prosperity serves as a reminder that, in economics, everything does affect everything else. Now that the basic framework has been presented for each topic—growth, business cycles and inflation—it's appropriate to consider the interaction among them.

Chapter 14

Growth, Cycles and the Value of Money
Putting It All Together

Growth and prosperity, business cycles and the value of money—these are the principal topics necessary for understanding how the economy works. Although our structure focuses on each of these topics separately, it is important to understand how they relate to each other.

Long-Term Interrelationships

Of the three topics considered, growth is by far the most important. An economy's growth path not only determines living standards, it also provides a long-term target for how fast spending can increase without a change in the value of money. If an economy's growth path amounts to three percent per year, it means that the economy is capable of producing three percent more output each year. Over time, as long as spending also increases by three percent each year, the total increase in spending will be matched by an increase in output, and prices will remain stable.

There is, of course, no guarantee that spending will increase at the same rate as the economy's ability to grow. Remember, spending in any economy depends on only two things: money and the rate at which it is exchanged. If money were increasing at three percent a year and the turnover in money were such that spending grew three percentage points faster than the monetary increase, then spending would increase by six percent each year. In this example, spending is rising twice as fast as the economy is able to increase output. As a result, half of the increase in spending will be made up of additional output, while the remainder will take the form of higher prices.

In order for price stability to exist, spending has to increase at the same rate at which the economy produces output. The ideal way to achieve such stability would be to boost the economy's growth path. In the example used, increasing the economy's growth path to 6 percent per year would suffice. Lower tax rates and reduced barriers to free markets might help accomplish this feat. However, if these policies have been adopted and 3 percent is total economic growth, then the road to price stability involves reducing the growth in spending to match the growth in output. This would occur if either the turnover in money slowed so that spending was rising no faster than the 3 percent growth in money, or if money failed to increase. Since the pace at which money turns over is not readily controllable, price stability is more likely to depend on stopping the growth in money than on influencing its turnover.

Short-Term Interrelationships

Once an economy's growth trend has been established, there is no guarantee that spending will increase at any set rate. The chapter on business cycles demonstrated how spending could rise or fall abruptly as a result of a change either in money or the rate at which it turns over. When spending does change abruptly, the economy's actual output can temporarily swing above or below its longer-term trend. It's possible for output to go above its longer-term trend because economies seldom operate at their maximum physical capabilities. Output usually can be increased by overtime work, the use of less skilled workers and by the extended operation of machines. Alternatively, output can be reduced by layoffs and shutting down machines.

At any point in time, shifts in spending can lead an economy to produce output that is close to or far from its longer-term growth path. This is because the value of money tends to change only gradually over time. Sam the counterfeiter's neighbors did not realize that his newly created spending was not matched by an equal creation of output; the same holds true for the economy as a whole. When spending begins to rise rapidly or to slump, it is not immediately apparent whether the change is the result of real economic forces or money. It often takes an extended period of time—perhaps as long as several years—before it becomes widely recognized that the value of money, and not the forces of real growth, have changed. Until that becomes apparent, workers and businesses react to changes in spending as if those changes resulted from real forces. As a result, when spending first changes, it is output and not prices that tends to swing the most.

In the extreme, a sharp drop in the money supply, such as occurred in the early 1930s, will reduce spending and output to the point where an economy is producing only a fraction of what it is capable of producing. Since prices tend to adjust slowly, it can take an extended period of time before the value of money fully adjusts to a drop in the money supply. Similarly, when the money supply is increased rapidly, as it was in the mid-1930s, real output can soar while money temporarily retains its value. The shifts in spending that produce business cycles will result in an economy that strays from its growth path from time to time. Only over extended periods of time will the value of money tend to adjust fully to the difference between the growth in spending and the economy's long-term growth path.

Cyclical vs. Longer-Term Forces

Distinguishing between cyclical forces, such as a change in the money supply, and longer-term forces, such as tax policy and the degree of freedom in markets, can be helpful in classifying information and simplifying an analysis. Furthermore, recognition that a development is essentially cyclical often suggests that it may soon be reversed. This is true whether it refers to a temporary sales boom or to a slump in business activity. However, a more fundamental problem with the economy's growth path signals a more serious, longer-lasting potential for poor performance. Even so, we must avoid being a slave to our structure. Cyclical policies can be so bad that they lead to chronic long-term problems. And abrupt changes in tax policies, or in the degree of freedom in markets, can provide for frequent shifts in an economy's growth path, thereby affecting the magnitude of business cycles.

Carried to an extreme, an ideal money policy—one that minimized the magnitude of any business fluctuations and produced price stability—could be expected to promote stability and efficiency, thus contributing to economic growth. In contrast, an abominable money policy—one characterized by hyper-inflation and erratic periods of booms and busts— holds the potential to destroy or severely limit output. When management or mismanagement of cyclical policies approaches these extremes, monetary policy holds the potential to become an even more powerful influence on long-term growth than free markets or taxes. However, under more normal circumstances, money has only a transitory impact on growth.

Just as extreme changes in monetary policy can influence an economy's growth path, extreme changes in free markets and tax rates can influence the shape of the business cycle. At the beginning of the Great Depression, Congress passed the highly destructive Smoot-Hawley tariff legislation and followed it in 1932 with the largest tax increase in U.S. history. Since these changes had a negative influence on the economy's growth path, they undoubtedly added to the severity of the cyclical collapse. More recently, tax increases in the late 1970s and into 1981 made inflation and any business downturns more serious than they would have been. In contrast, the tax cuts that took effect in 1982 and 1983 raised the economy's growth path and contributed to more real growth and lower inflation than monetary policy alone could have produced.

In an economy experiencing strong increases in productivity, an erratic monetary policy will still lead to a boom-bust pattern of spending. However, as the accompanying chart shows, the "bust" may consist of no more than a leveling-off of activity. In an economy with no growth, the same monetary policy mistakes would result in a major recession. Once the elements of growth have been tampered with to such an extent that an economy is in a state of economic decline, even a stable monetary policy would be capable of achieving nothing more than a smooth, orderly deterioration in living standards.

BUSINESS CYCLES

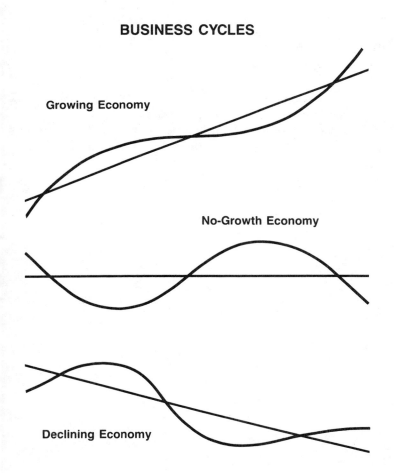

Growing Economy

No-Growth Economy

Declining Economy

Putting It All Together

In economics, everything does affect everything else, and the interrelationship among so many factors can be confusing. Some confusion can be avoided by examining separately the nature of growth, cycles and the value of money—and the forces that affect each. However, it's also important to realize that categorizing the major issues into three topics is solely for the purpose of organizing information. Without such an approach, it becomes difficult—if not impossible, to manage the flood of economic information that otherwise threatens to inundate us. Even so, the policies influencing growth, cycles and the value of money are inextricably interrelated, and those interrelationships must be recognized.

Now that the structure for how the economy operates has been developed, identified and explained, it's time to deal with some of the more popular topics in economics: deficits, interest rates, the rest of the world, and the morality of economic systems.

Book 3

Key Topics
in Economics

Chapter 15

Those Despicable Deficits

Nowhere does voodoo economics dance with such vigor as it does in many of the contemporary discussions of deficits and interest rates. In the early 1970s we heard the incessant chants cursing the debt crisis facing state and local governments. Several years later, the chants concentrated on the corporations tumbling head over heels into debt. By the early 1980s, state and local and corporate debt problems seemed to fade away only to be replaced by those of the federal government. Nor was the international area to escape the hysteria. In 1982 and 1983 concern focused on massive Third World debts to the U.S. By 1984, the focus shifted again. This time there was growing consternation over U.S. debt to the rest of the world. It often seems all too tempting to join the crowd and jump on the bandwagon of hysteria that surrounds deficits. After all, if debt is bad, and more debt is worse, then massive deficits must be the work of Satan himself. Perhaps. But before embarking on a crusade against demonic deficits, it's useful to consider some fairly basic issues surrounding deficits: What exactly is a deficit? Is it good or bad? What impact does it have on the economy? Why all the hysteria?

Establishing the Structure

Our structure for investigating how the economy works involves three major topics: growth, cycles and the value of money. When considering other topics, such as deficits and interest rates, it's helpful to understand how they relate within that structure. In some cases, they will relate to all of the major topics. The price system is one such example. Prices are part of the market system and, as such, they provide essential information to assure an efficient use of resources for growth. Prices also respond in different ways at various stages of business cycles. And finally, prices are an integral part of the value of money. In a similar manner, deficits and interest rates relate to each of these major topics.

When deficits and interest rates are described, it will become apparent that they are a logical outgrowth of free markets. They behave differently at different stages of a business cycle, and the value of money plays an important role in their determination. Most important of all, whereas free markets, tax rates and money represent the initiating forces that influence growth, cycles and the value of money, deficits and interest rates are among the consequences of these factors.

What is a Deficit?—Identifying the Issue

At one time or another everyone experiences a deficit. It occurs whenever someone spends more income than they earned for a certain period of time. Deficits are a natural by-product of a free market system. Such a system not only permits individuals to decide what to buy with the income they earn, but it also gives them the option to buy more or less then they have earned. They do this through the process of debt and credit.

Here's how it works. Whenever individuals produce something that will be sold to others, they do so for the income they receive. The value of the income they receive for producing the product is equal to the market value of the product produced. Hence, a dollar of income corresponds to each dollar of output produced in any period. As a result, the income people earn gives them a claim to an equal amount of output produced elsewhere in the economy. Some people find that it is in their interest to claim more output than is justified by the income they earned in a particular period. This usually occurs when someone buys a house or other expensive item. Others often find it in their interest to post-pone some of their claims to the economy's output. As a result, they can enjoy more output than their income would allow at some time in the future. The process of transferring current claims to the economy's output for future claims increases the value of that income by making it conform more closely to each person's desires. In this way it enhances incentives to produce and thereby promotes growth and prosperity.

Since total income always equals total output, the only way anyone can claim more output than they earn is if someone else agrees to spend less than they earn. Such agreements occur all the time. Those claiming more of the economy's out-put during a certain period are borrowers or debtors, and the amount they borrow represents their debt or deficit for that period. Those giving up their claim to present output are lenders, creditors, or savers, and the amount they lend is their credit, surplus or saving for that period. In return for giving up the use of some of their current income, savers receive a claim to the borrowers' future income. The amount of the claim is related to the interest rate (more about this in the next chapter).

While individuals or organizations can go into debt, society as a whole cannot. The reason for this is simple. Society as a whole cannot consume more than it has produced. Hence, society as a whole can never go into debt. Only individuals, organizations or parts of society can incur debt. And, they can incur debt (place a greater claim on output than they have earned) only to the extent that other individuals agree to save (give up their present claim to output).

In and of themselves, deficits are neither good nor bad. The main consideration in a decision to incur debt should be whether or not debtors will experience future benefits from their purchases that exceed their future expense in paying off their debt. So long as the ongoing benefit from driving a car or living in a house will exceed the ongoing cost of the debt incurred to buy those items, then going into debt is worthwhile.

The same axiom holds true with respect to a business. Is it imprudent for a business to borrow $200 million? There is no way to provide a meaningful answer to this question without having additional information on the size of the business, the growth in the demand for its products, the use of the $200 million and so on. The deciding factor, as in the case of the individual, is whether the benefits from the decision to borrow exceed the costs. More specifically, if the profits from the use of the borrowed funds exceed the costs of borrowing, then going into debt is justified. The more the profits resulting from deficit financing exceed the costs, the greater the justification for going into debt. A highly success-ful, growing business may be justified in increasing the size of its deficit each year. However, since all debt involves a judg-ment concerning future developments, both borrowers and lenders need to be cautious. Should future circumstances unfold in an unexpected manner, what once appeared pru-dent may quickly prove to be imprudent.

There is a widespread notion that when the federal govern-ment runs a deficit, it is automatically creating more money. This notion is wrong. Government debt follows the same basic principles as private debt, and a government's decision to engage in deficit financing should be based on similar reason-ing. In the government's case, the cost of deficit financing represents an implicit tax on the future income of its citizens. When it runs a deficit, a government commits to future taxes to pay for the interest and principal on the debt. Whe-ther or not a government is justified in pursuing deficit financ-ing depends on whether or not the ongoing benefits to future taxpayers exceed the ongoing costs in terms of interest and principal. If a government engages in deficit financing to build a school, this is clearly a case where—since future tax-payers will experience some of the benefit from the building—they should pay some of the costs. Clearly, deficit financing for capital items (buildings, roads, dams) can be just as prudent for a government as for a private business. In an ideal world, the government would calculate a separate budget for these capital items. While the part of its budget representing expenses for current services should be in balance, the capital budget could show a deficit. So long as the deficit was consistent with the requirement that the increase in benefits to future taxpayers matched the increase in their tax burdens, the deficits would be prudent.

Unfortunately, the world of politics falls somewhat short of the ideal. As a result, it's difficult (perhaps impossible) to view federal deficits from any idealistic vantage point. However, it is important to understand that there is nothing inherently wrong with deficits. In an ideal world, federal deficits may not only be appropriate, but in a growing, prospering economy, a policy calling for progressively larger deficits each year *could be* the most desirable policy of all.

What Role Do Deficits Play?—Deficit Theory

Much of the confusion surrounding the issue of deficits arises because of a misunderstanding of the meaning of debt. As already indicated, deficits are a natural consequence of free markets. Deficits arise from the desire to increase the value of our income by shifting our claims to output from one period to another. Since others must agree to save (postpone their claims to output) before any deficits can occur, a theory of deficits can just as equally be termed a theory of surpluses.

Prior to this century, the economic literature surrounding deficits and surpluses was in a state of total confusion. This condition changed in 1906 when Irving Fisher published *The Nature of Capital and Income*. In this book, Fisher explains why the economic literature was so confusing and proceeds to explain the nature of debt and saving. Fisher's book cleared up the confusion surrounding these issues. Unfortunately, when economists left the well-traveled path of traditional economic thought and embarked on virgin Keynesian soil, many of Fisher's insights were lost. From the economists' new perspective, spending was viewed as being fundamentally different from saving. Saving was mistakenly viewed as a failure to spend. Hence, spending was viewed as a stimulus to business activity, while saving was assumed to have the opposite effect. The more that was spent, the greater the stimulus was thought to be. If government ran a deficit, spending more than it took in, it was viewed as driving the economy forward. The same went for the private sector. Spend and you stimulate business, save and you help sink it.

This view regarding the impact of spending and deficits represented a new idea. Since economics deals with issues that are essential to our lives, at one time or another every thinking person believes they have discovered some new insights into how the system operates. When such revelations occur to renowned experts, armchair insights often become an integral part of conventional wisdom. It's somewhat sad and unfortunate to realize that one of the few things many students remember from their economics classes—that deficits stimulate while surpluses restrain—is wrong. The view never had any prominence in the traditions of economic thought prior to Keynes, and there has been no evidence since to support it.

Since the only way a deficit can exist is if someone offers to save an amount equal to the deficit, the view that deficits stimulate while saving restrains activity is odd. Should some people decide that they would like to spend more than they have earned, the interest rate—or price of credit—will rise so that others will be encouraged to spend less. Why this process should be expected to stimulate the economy was never clearly examined. In fact, after more than forty years of teaching that deficits stimulate the economy, in the early 1980s many economists made a slight adjustment to their views on the role of deficits. Deficits were no longer seen as stimulating the economy, rather, they were viewed as restraining spending. (Well, "slight adjustment" may understate the case.) The new reasoning was at least as curious as the earlier view. Recognizing that deficits might actually raise interest rates, some observers began to argue that deficits did, in effect, restrain the economy. Still others had an even more curious insight. Deficits still stimulate, they argued, but the stimulus can be so great that the fear of future inflation actually drives up interest rates today, thereby restraining the economy. Such groping and ad hoc adjustments to a theory strongly resemble the practice of voodoo.

Just as there is a grain of truth in the argument that deficits may stimulate the economy, there is also the same grain of truth that they may restrain it. The real issue concerning deficits is whether or not they are a major force in initiating changes in growth, business cycles or inflation. In fact, they are nothing of the kind. Deficits are the consequence of a whole host of economic forces. While the behavior and impact of those factors that produce a deficit can be extremely important, the deficit itself is not.

To illustrate this point consider Mr. Frivil, an individual who habitually runs a balanced budget. However, in the process he spends money like a drunken sailor. Each and every whim that comes along is fulfilled. Moreover, one of the reasons his budget is in balance is because each year Frivil sells some of his assets to cover his frivolous expenses. While Frivil has a balanced budget, he is not behaving in a responsible manner. In addition to being frivolous, his wealth is rapidly declining and his financial future is in jeopardy.

Frivil's counterpart is a Miss B. Wright, who has brought her spending well under control. However, she happens to be running a deficit of ten percent of her income each year. This deficit results from her borrowing funds to attend night school to improve her skills so that in the future she'll be able to earn more income. For anyone to claim that Miss B. Wright is behaving in an irresponsible manner just because she is running a deficit of ten percent of her income is, well, irresponsible.

A good accountant will object that Frivil's budget isn't really balanced since the income he gets from selling his assets reduces his wealth. And, to view his financial position in a meaningful way, the change in wealth should be noted in addition to his income and spending. The accountant is correct in assuming that to be meaningful, a deficit or surplus should be related to the impact it has on the change in wealth. But what this really tells us is that, alone, the deficit or surplus simply is not a very meaningful concept.

In the late 1970s the U.S. federal government was behaving much as Mr. Frivil. Spending rose rapidly—fifteen percent a year—and the budget deficit was reduced. The reason the deficit shrunk was the government rapidly increased its tax receipts. Such reduction in the deficit didn't reflect responsible behavior. Since the funds the government took to help balance its budget were funds that could have been used for growth and productivity improvement, its behavior might be considered akin to cashing in its assets. The end result should have been a stagnant economy, with higher inflation and higher interest rates, and that's just what occurred. But you never would have realized it by focusing on the rapidly shrinking federal budget deficit.

In the early 1980s the federal government's situation moved closer to that of Miss B. Wright. By 1984 government spending slowed to about half the rate of increase of the late 1970s, in spite of some sharp increases in spending for defense, unemployment and farm programs. However, as a result of lower tax rates and less inflation, tax receipts showed only modest increases. The offset was that the private sector got to keep more of the funds that would have gone to government. In a static analysis, nothing much would happen. The larger deficit would be offset by government borrowing, and the public's future tax burden would be higher. But the economy is not static—it's dynamic. At lower tax rates, incentives to innovate and to utilize savings more efficiently give rise to better productivity performance and greater output.

A deficit incurred by tax cuts in an overtaxed economy represents an investment in future growth. Much like borrowing to attend night school, the end result will be a strong potential for greater income and wealth, not just for one individual, but for an entire nation.

The debate in the early 1980s over federal deficits was entirely misdirected. In economics the real issue is growth, not deficits. Had the underlying productivity trend in the U.S. from 1979-81 continued to 1991, U.S. output in 1991 would amount to $4.3 trillion in 1985 dollars. Instead, on the basis of the productivity path evident from 1981-84, output would be $5.1 trillion by 1991. Hence, the difference between the poor productivity trend prior to 1981 and the more encouraging trend since that time represents a difference of $800 billion of output a year by 1991. This amounts to an additional $6,500 per year for each worker in 1991. If the additional output were to be taxed at a rate of 20 percent, it would represent an additional $160 billion per year in actual goods and services that would be available for use by the government to clean the environment, help the poor, bolster defense, or retire government debt.

Note that with the additional growth, the entire nation benefits. This is true whether the growth in productivity is accompanied by a balanced federal budget, a massive deficit, or a massive surplus. The essential economic issue is growth, not deficits. Without growth, the issue of balancing the federal budget involves a debate over who owes what to whom out of a fixed pie. The citizens of the Latin American countries have substantially less debt per capita than those in the U.S. They are not heard praising the wisdom of past policymakers for leaving them with such a dubious distinction. The real proof of prudent economic policy is not the magnitude of debt that is left to future generations, but the productiveness of their economic environment.

In the end, the significance of a deficit, whether it belongs to an individual, a company, a country or a government is far more complex than simply looking at some dollar figure and trying to resolve whether it's good or bad. As the consequence of many factors, a deficit may be the result of either good or bad policies or favorable or unfavorable developments. The same may be said for a surplus or a balanced budget. In either case, it's impossible to make a judgment about its merits or demerits without focusing on more substantive issues such as the behavior of spending and income, and the ultimate impact these will have on the future performance of the economy.

What Are Balance of Payments Deficits?

The confusion over the role of debt in the domestic economy is often confounded when the focus shifts to international issues. For this reason it's instructive to consider the debt issues from this perspective. It has been mentioned that any entity can incur a deficit. When that entity is an entire country the deficit is often termed a balance of payments deficit. While some of the details or implications of a country's debt may differ from that of an individual, the essence of understanding its significance remains the same. For each family, individual, community or country, an account can be drawn up to show their excess spending over income for any given period. If this account shows that more was spent than earned, then some other group must have loaned it the funds to accomplish this feat. Each entity will then have an account showing how much it spent in excess of its income for that period and a second account showing how much it borrowed. This first account—spending in excess of income—when applied to a whole community is referred to as its balance of payments or, more specifically, its balance of payments on current account.

One way to make such an impressive and scholarly sounding phrase as "balance of payments on current account" a part of your everyday vocabulary is to calculate such an account for your own family. Simply total all your income for one time period, such as a year, and subtract all spending during that same period. Now if you happen to be a student, or if you happened to purchase a house during the year, your "balance of payments on current account" will probably look disastrous. Don't panic! If you were a country, your balance of payments condition might be front page news. In fact, the publicity surrounding your massive deficit might force your finance minister to resign. However, as an individual, you realize that you incurred this deficit by taking out a student loan or a mortgage. What this means is that you gave up some of your future claims to the economy's output to someone who apparently decided that your future earning power was likely to be sufficient to enable you to repay the loan.

If your balance of payments account is in deficit, meaning you spent more on the economy's output than you earned, then others must have spent less than they earned. The only way you can purchase more of the economy's output than you earned is if someone else agreed to give you some of what they earned. Stated differently, your deficit must be offset by someone else's surplus. And, your deficit on current account must be offset by a surplus on your capital account. The capital account simply tells where you obtained the funds to spend more than you earned. In the case of our student, her capital account would show a surplus or positive increase in funds equal to her student loan.

Just as in the case of an individual, we can calculate the balance of payments for all who live in a particular city or country. The meaning of such a measure can be extremely difficult to interpret. If the country's economy is young and developing, the businessmen and government may need to borrow huge amounts from other countries to take full advantage of that development. Also, a mature economy undergoing an economic revival may attract foreign investment and run large balance of payments deficits. Also, an economy whose individuals have accumulated assets (claims to output) may decide to exercise those claims, much as a retired couple would do. The result again would be a substantial balance of payments deficit.

Why All the Hysteria?

One of the most fascinating developments in recent years has been the ongoing hysteria surrounding deficits. Once the nature of deficits is examined, it becomes obvious that there may be little, if any, economic basis for all the fuss. There is, however, a political basis. Both conservatives and liberals often believe it's in their best interest when the public's wrath is directed toward federal deficits. Conservatives approve of fostering deficit mania since they believe it will help in their primary objective—reducing government spending. Liberals approve of deficit mania in their quest for the opposite— higher taxes to pay for more government spending.

Emphasizing deficit phobia not only plays nicely into the hands of politicians of different persuasions, but it's also advantageous to those at the Federal Reserve Board. Every Fed Chairman is under enormous pressure to depict deficits as a scourge upon the economy. By doing so, he can effectively direct attention (and criticism) away from monetary policy—and away from the Fed.

An unfortunate outgrowth of deficit mania has been its effect on different groups. Many observers, failing to recognize the economic or political rationale surrounding the issue, have been caught up in the whirlwind of hysteria. Having listened to the incessant stream of arguments against deficits, they have joined the chorus.

The main conclusion to reach in assessing the significance of deficits is to be cautious in reaching any conclusions. Deficits are not demonic. They often serve an important role in increasing the efficiency and flexibility of choice. There is no way that anyone can look at a deficit and conclude that it is good or bad, or that it will impact the economy in any specific way. An increase in a federal deficit that results from a frivolous increase in government spending will have a different impact from one that results from lower tax rates. And a deficit that results from lower tax rates in an over-taxed economy will have different effects than a deficit that results from tax cuts in an under-taxed economy. A deficit that results from a downturn in business activity will have still a different impact.

The same is true for trade deficits. A trade deficit that results from an increase in money and a short-term burst in domestic spending will have different implications than one that results from attracting foreign investment. And a trade deficit that results primarily from a sharp deterioration in investment prospects abroad would have still different implications. To imply that deficits by themselves have any effect at all without referring to the reasons for the deficit is a prime example of economic voodoo. Before condemning a deficit and rushing to solve the next deficit crisis, the behavior of the key components of a deficit—spending and income—should be carefully examined. The burden of the deficit should be viewed in terms of the wealth that the group has built up, its potential for future income, and a host of other relevant factors. Only after these are considered can the real significance of any deficit be grasped.

Chapter 16

Interest Rates

Closely related to deficits is one of the most fascinating topics in economics—the rate of interest. As will become apparent, the rate of interest provides a link between present and future economic activity. In this sense interest rates have important implications for the performance of any investment. In contrast to deficits, the widespread attention devoted to interest rates is well-deserved.

The Rate of Interest—Identifying the Issue

The interest rate is the price associated with shifting claims to the economy's output from one time period to another. Savers or lenders are willing to give up some of their claims to the economy's present output in return for someone else's claims in the future. Debtors or borrowers are on the other side of the transaction. They want to control more of the economy's output in the present than their income will allow, and in return must give up some of their claims to future output. The interest rate provides lenders with some idea of the amount of future claims they will receive, and borrowers with some idea of how much future output they have agreed to give up. However, the rate of interest does not give savers or borrowers a precise idea of how much future output is involved in their agreement because of the many unknowns surrounding the future.

What Determines Interest Rates?—Interest Rate Theory

Most economists will say that interest rates are determined by the supply and demand for credit and debt. This is true, but not very helpful. Supply and demand is a catch-all phrase that includes all the possible determinants. It would have been technically correct to deal with all the major issues previously considered in the same manner. Growth depends on the supply and demand for real output; business cycles, on the supply and demand for spending; and the value of money, on the supply and demand for money. True, but not very useful. The real challenge of any theory is to choose those forces that tend to dominate supply and demand.

Historical Foundations

In order to focus on the key determinants of interest rates, it's necessary to have a clear understanding of the issues involved. From a historical perspective, the economic literature on interest rates suffered some of the same confusion that surrounded the issue of debt and credit, as well as some additional confusion. As with debt and credit, the issues were cleared up at the turn of the century by Irving Fisher. His classic work, appropriately titled *The Rate of Interest* and published in 1907, is the best and perhaps the only book that clearly and comprehensively discusses what can be an extremely complex topic.

Unfortunately, two developments occurred that have since contributed to losing many of Fisher's insights. First, Fisher rewrote his 1907 book. At the request of many economists, who suggested how he might better explain his topic, Fisher produced *The Theory of Interest* in 1930. This second book, an abbreviated version of the earlier one, is more difficult to understand. Instead of accomplishing his objective of reaching more people, Fisher accomplished the opposite. His 1930 book replaced the earlier one and, as a result, *The Rate of Interest* has been out of print for many years. The failure of many economists to read the original work has contributed to much of today's confusion surrounding interest rates.

The second development that caused many of Fisher's insights to be abandoned stemmed from the Keynesian influence. Many of Keynes' followers confused the rate of interest with the price of money (see Chapter 12) and frequently viewed interest rates as an initiating factor instead of a consequence of economic forces. Both of these mistakes changed the focus on interest rates away from those insights provided by Fisher and back to the confusion that preceded him.

Explanation

Fisher's contributions to understanding debt and credit formed the basis for his insights to the rate of interest. Since the rate of interest involves a unique time dimension, its determinants relate to those factors that influence the value of claims to future output relative to current output. These include the expected value of money and expected taxes, which help to identify accurately the value of future claims. They also include increases in productivity and saving patterns, which influence the way people value real after-tax output in the future. In addition, monetary policies can temporarily alter the real after-tax rate of interest. Finally, there is the element of risk, which creates different interest rates for different instruments. And these are only the *key* determinants of rates. There are others as well. Understanding interest rates is not only a major challenge, it may well be economics' answer to that great philosophical inquiry—where's the beef?

In explaining the determinants of interest rates, three major components are considered: the tax premium, inflation premium, and real after-tax component. Each of these will be considered in turn.

Tax Premium

An important but often ignored component of the interest rate is the tax premium. Both parties to the credit transaction are (or should be) thinking of the real claims to output that they will actually pay or receive. If future interest payments are tax deductible, then this reduces the amount of future claims to output that borrowers will have to give up at a given interest rate. As a result, for any given investment, the higher the tax rate borrowers expect, the higher the interest rate they are willing to pay.

Similar reasoning is used by savers. Since they are parting with claims to real output today, they are naturally concerned with the claims they will receive in the future. If savers expect high taxes on interest income, then the amount of future real output they can expect at today's interest rate is lower than it would be in a low-tax environment. As a result, in a high-tax environment savers will demand a higher interest rate for providing the same amount of savings they would have in a low-tax environment. Hence, so long as tax rates impact the claims to output implied in the agreement between savers and borrowers, higher tax rates will serve to raise interest rates directly.

Inflation Premium

The interest rate is a unique price in that it attempts to indicate the amount of future claims to output that will exchange hands. However, savers and borrowers do not agree to exchange future output; rather, they agree to exchange money. In order to determine how much of a claim to future output is involved in their agreement, both savers and borrowers must consider the impact of a change in the value of money on their agreement. For example, if they expect ten percent inflation over the life of their agreement, they will adjust the interest rate accordingly by ten percent. If they're right and inflation is ten percent, the ten percent adjustment in interest rates will offset the ten percent decline in the value of money each year so that, at the end of the period, the money paid back is worth the same in terms of a claim to output as it was when the saver first gave it up.

In the real world, neither the saver nor borrower can be certain how inflation will affect the real value of their agreement. If inflation is more than they expected, savers lose because they are repaid in money that provides them with claims to output that are worth less than they anticipated. Borrowers, who have to give up claims to output that are worth less than expected, are the winners. Should inflation be lower than expected, the tables are reversed: borrowers lose and savers win.

Uncertainty over inflation will make savers and borrowers extremely nervous. They may change their assessment of inflation quickly or slowly, as the situation dictates. Still, amid all the uncertainty over the future value of money, they will attempt as best they can to incorporate their expectations into the rate of interest. These expectations add a premium—an inflationary premium—over and above the real after-tax portion of the interest rate. Depending on the importance of the inflationary environment, this may be the most significant factor affecting the interest rate.

By adjusting the interest rate for inflationary and tax expectations, lenders and borrowers are changing their contract to have it reflect more closely the real value of the money they expect to pay or receive. Once these factors have been accounted for, what remains is the real after-tax rate of interest—the rate that reflects the real value of future output that borrowers expect to pay and lenders expect to receive.

Real After-Tax Rate

Debt and credit involve the transfer of the use of income through time. The main purpose for using income stems from the services we gain from its use. And the use of services today is worth more than the use of those services at some point in the future.

To see why this is so, imagine someone offering to give you either $100,000 worth of income today or the equivalent of $100,000 worth of income a year from now. We will always choose the use of income today over its use in the future. By taking the $100,000 and buying a house today, as opposed to buying the same house a year from now, we enjoy the services provided by the house for an additional year. These extra services explain why income today is more valuable than income in the future. This is the basic principle behind the payment of interest. It means that in addition to repaying the equivalent in income borrowed, there is a need for some additional compensation. This additional compensation is reflected in the real after-tax portion of the interest rate.

Productivity Growth

There are many factors that influence the real after-tax portion of interest. One of these is the productivity trend. If productivity is not increasing and the average investment in an economy yields no real return for an additional dollar spent, then it will not pay the average investor to borrow money at a positive real after-tax rate of interest. To do so would involve a poor business decision. It would involve paying back more claims to future output than would be received from the investment.

Even with an average return on investment of zero, there will be some opportunities for a positive return, and investors in these areas can afford to pay a positive real after-tax rate. While the average economy-wide return to an investment is not the sole factor determining the real after-tax rate of interest, it can have a powerful impact. If a large proportion of an economy's investment opportunities involve a zero return, the amount of borrowing at positive real after-tax interest rates will be greatly limited. In contrast, in an economy characterized by strong productivity, a wide variety of investment opportunities with substantial returns will exist. This means that a large number of investors will be both willing and able to incur relatively high real after-tax commitments to borrow funds.

Saving Patterns

In addition to productivity, a community's saving patterns hold the potential to impact significantly the real after-tax rate of interest. A community saves for the future when its individuals direct their resources to producing things that will enable future output to be greater. This includes spending on such items as machines, buildings and roads. Such saving patterns are influenced by a community's valuation of future income versus present income. Social factors and tradition may play an important role in determining how individuals in a particular economy value future income. A community that places a great deal of value on the future, or on meeting the needs of the next generation, will tend to save more at any given interest rate than a community of hedonists and playboys. Demographics may also have an impact on saving patterns. A community with either a very young or very old population with substantial immediate needs will tend to save far less than a community with a large population of people contemplating retirement. Those factors that encourage relatively large amounts of saving from current income serve to reduce real after-tax interest rates, while those that discourage saving will have the opposite effect.

Monetary Policy

Another factor impacting the real after-tax rate of interest stems from the effect of short-term swings in the creation of money. When the Federal Reserve Board purchases government securities (in an attempt to increase the growth in the money supply), it must offer a higher price for those securities than already exists in the marketplace. This has the effect of temporarily lowering real after-tax interest rates. Once business activity begins to rise in response to a relatively low real after-tax rate of interest, the rate will rise. This cyclical element in interest rates is a key factor influencing business cycles. It is the only element that many people consider when they associate high interest rates with tight money or low rates with easy or loose money. However, as we have seen, there may be any number of factors contributing to the behavior of interest rates other than those associated with the business cycle.

Government Deficits

Of all the potential forces impacting interest rates, deficits have recently received the most attention. This is unfortunate. While there is a grain of truth to the argument that large government deficits raise interest rates, that grain is extremely small.

In order to isolate the impact of a government deficit on interest rates it is necessary to allow for the impact of inflation, taxes, productivity, saving patterns, and monetary policy. Once this is done, the issue becomes trying to determine what role deficits play in influencing that portion of the real after-tax rate of interest that remains to be explained. By reducing the available private saving, the existence of a deficit, in and of itself, may reduce the opportunities for private investment by raising the interest rate. The extent of the increase depends on how sensitive investment is to a change in the real after-tax rate of interest. If investment projects are highly sensitive to rates, then a relatively small increase in interest rates would result from a change in deficits. The less sensitive investment projects are, the more the real after-tax interest rate will rise.

The important thing to keep in mind about the impact of deficits on interest rates is that its impact only affects the real after-tax portion of the rate. As we will see, in a high-inflation, high-tax environment this will be a relatively small portion of the total interest rate. Furthermore, the real after-tax interest rate is affected by many factors such as productivity performance and saving patterns. And finally, to the extent that the deficit "crowds out" private investment and lowers productivity growth, it actually creates pressure to reduce real after-tax interest rates! The great preoccupation with deficits and their impact on interest rates represents one of those many side roads that economic thought seems prone to travel from time to time.

Some observers believe that federal deficits play a key role in formulating inflationary expectations. While there may be some truth to this position, it is interesting to recall that those who agree with this view warned of high inflation for 1982, then 1983, then 1984, and then 1985. Those who heeded such warnings geared their investment strategies toward higher inflation. They borrowed funds in anticipation of higher interest rates, bought precious metals and other real assets and built up their inventories. Some financial institutions made loans under the assumption that higher prices would increase the value of their borrowers' assets. When the higher inflation did not materialize, all who expected it learned a very painful financial lesson. Such lessons are the type that turn investors into laborers. It is these lessons, not some economic theory, that eventually determine inflationary expectations.

To downplay the role of deficits in setting interest rates is not to negate the role of the government. Given the size and scope of government, its influence over the rate of interest is all-encompassing. Since government policies control inflation and taxes, government is obviously responsible for the inflation and tax premiums. In addition, its policies can directly or indirectly influence the real after-tax rate of interest. By impacting productivity, government policies can raise or lower the attractiveness of a whole range of investment opportunities in any economy. Furthermore, government holds the potential for affecting saving patterns. By creating an environment of peace and economic stability as opposed to strife and instability, government may indirectly influence the saving patterns in any community. And finally, through the Federal Reserve, the government's monetary policy will affect the cyclical pattern of interest rates.

Risk

The role of risk in determining interest rates is largely indeterminant. In setting the level of rates, the key factor is the response of savers and borrowers to a change in risk. If the economic environment becomes more uncertain, borrowers may reduce their willingness to borrow and interest rates will tend to decline. However, savers may either save more as a hedge against uncertainty (in which case rates would decline further) or they may save less due to the uncertainty of future income (in which case rates would go up).

Risk tends to be more important in determining the relationship among different interest rates than in setting the overall-level of rates. For example, in a highly uncertain climate where savers fear a default by debtors, they will attempt to shift their claims to short-term, relatively safe securities. This preference will tend to lower the rate of interest on those securities, while increasing the rates on securities viewed as less secure.

The concern over risk may be either the risk of outright default or partial default. If future inflation is higher than expected, the saver suffers from what amounts to a partial default. In either case, these risks increase as the time period is extended. As a result, long-term interest rates tend to be higher than short-term rates. And the greater the uncertainty regarding the future, the greater the difference between them.

Evidence—Measuring the Determinants of Interest Rates

To suggest that economics has unraveled the mystery surrounding interest rates simply means that there is a basic understanding of the main determinants. It does not necessarily mean that anyone knows for sure whether an interest rate of ten percent is high or low, or even what portion of that rate represents the real after-tax component. The measurement of the different components of interest rates has been hampered not only by the complexity of the problem, but also by the failure of many researchers to understand the nature of the problem. Trying, as some have done, to explain the behavior of inflation-adjusted interest rates without identifying the tax premium is an obvious exercise in futility. In spite of a failure to develop anything but the crudest measures of the determinants of interest rates, the crucial role played by interest rates makes it important to make the attempt.

Tax Premium

The first adjustment to rates should isolate the tax premium. This premium reflects the tax rates that borrowers and savers expect will impact the amount of dollars actually paid or received over the time period considered in their interest rate agreement. Although there are many difficulties in measuring any type of expectations, there are some reasonable approaches. One method is to base expectations of future taxes on recent experience. The main thing to keep in mind with this assumption is that recent tax rates may not always capture expectations about future tax rates. A tax hike that everyone expects, but has not yet occurred, will by definition raise the tax premium. However, an approach that uses past or current tax rates will not reflect the higher premium.

A second problem in measuring the tax premium is identifying the appropriate tax rates. As discussed in the chapter on taxes, there has been relatively little work in this area. As a result, we will use the previously mentioned Harris series on effective marginal tax rates. This series estimates an effective marginal tax rate of 32 percent for 1984. If this accurately reflects the tax on additional interest income as expected by savers and investors, then the tax premium on a 13 percent bond in 1984 would have amounted to approximately 4 percentage points.

A further check on the magnitude of the tax premium is simply to measure the difference between tax-exempt interest rates and taxable rates. While there are factors other than the tax premium that can influence this spread, the figures do suggest that with interest rates at 13 percent the tax environment in 1984 was contributing close to 4 percentage points to those rates.

Inflation Premium

As with taxes, the inflation premium in interest rates should reflect expected inflation over the life of the agreement. Little is known about the formation or change in such expectations. As a result, any measure is bound to be fairly crude and a somewhat inadequate proxy for the real thing. Most measures base inflationary expectations on recent inflation experience. For 1984, such a measure produces estimates of 5 to 6 percent for expected inflation, close to the results of various surveys.

Real After-Tax Rate

Removing the tax and inflation premiums produces an estimate of the real after-tax rate of interest. For early 1984 this rate was estimated to be close to 2 to 3 percent. Using the procedures noted above, the pattern for interest rates over the past twenty-five years is shown on the following page.

The estimated real after-tax interest rate in 1984 was close to where it was in the 1960s. However, for the late 1970s and early 1980s, the rate was negative. While this may simply reflect a bad estimate of the expected tax or inflation environment, it is interesting to note that the movement in the real after-tax rate corresponds to the general deterioration and subsequent revival of productivity growth during this period. This provides some tentative reason to suggest that productivity performance may be a more powerful force impacting real after-tax interest rates than saving patterns. Until more extensive research is conducted into tax rates and the nature and formation of inflationary and tax expectations, any further conclusion would be pure speculation.

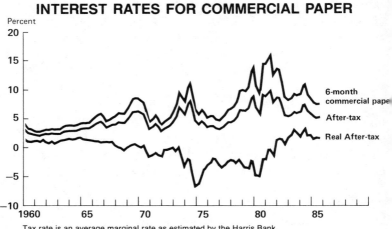

INTEREST RATES FOR COMMERCIAL PAPER

Tax rate is an average marginal rate as estimated by the Harris Bank.
Real rates are after-tax rates minus a 1-year average of inflation.
Source: Harris Bank

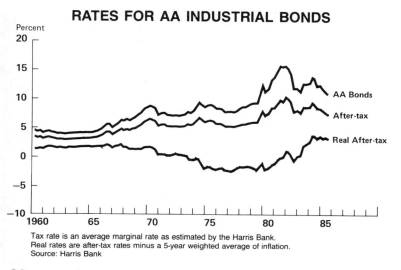

RATES FOR AA INDUSTRIAL BONDS

Tax rate is an average marginal rate as estimated by the Harris Bank.
Real rates are after-tax rates minus a 5-year weighted average of inflation.
Source: Harris Bank

Observation

As in other areas, observation is important to furthering our knowledge of interest rates and the factors that determine them. However, for observation to proceed in a meaningful way it must start with a framework. And the one provided by Irving Fisher over three quarters of a century ago remains the most fruitful. Providing rough measures for the components of interest rates is an important step toward discovering why rates are where they are and why they change.

Since many of today's economists are not familiar with Fisher's contributions, their statements about interest rates are often steeped in confusion. In explaining economic developments, interest rates cannot be viewed, as so many insist on doing, as an initiating force. The reason for this should now be apparent. A decline in interest rates that results from an increase in the money supply would have totally different implications for the economy than a decline that results from a deterioration in productivity. And lower interest rates that resulted from a lower tax premium would have still different implications. Starting an analysis with a change in interest rates instead of with the reason for the change is voodoo—pure and simple.

157

Chapter 17

What in the World is Going On?

Economics can be extremely confusing even when only one economy is being considered. When the focus shifts to the international sphere, confusion is often raised to new heights. This alone provides sufficient reason to understand international economics. For when a subject provides fertile ground for sowing confusion, special interests can be counted on to spread the fertilizer in promoting their own cause. There are other more positive reasons for trying to grasp the essence of international economics. First and foremost is the fact that we live and work in a world economy. As such, the interaction among different economies is important to the operation of any particular economy. To place such interaction in perspective, it's useful to consider how it relates to the structure developed earlier. When approached in this way, it's easier to see the extent to which international economics is merely a logical extension of the economics considered in earlier chapters and the extent to which it has an entirely different dimension.

Interaction Among Economies—Growth and Prosperity

Too often, the public perceives international economics as an issue of "them" versus "us." This provincial approach to the subject is not very meaningful. In a narrow sense it can just as easily be reformulated to focus on each of us as in-dividuals or families versus the rest of humanity. In a broader sense, it can be the interaction of all humanity against the elements. Precisely what constitutes "them" and what con-stitutes "us" is a distinction best made by philosophers, religious fanatics, politicians or racists. In viewing the situa-tion from an economic viewpoint, political boundaries, religion, race or many of the other potential distinctions between "them" and "us" are simply not valid. In order to understand what are valid distinctions, it's helpful to under-stand the economic relationship between an individual or small group and their surrounding community.

A family that is truly self-sufficient would produce every-thing necessary for its survival. Each person within the family has to be a "Jack-of-all-trades," with little potential for develop-ing special skills. So long as the family is self-sufficient, it's not affected by events outside of its immediate area. An inflation or monetary disturbance in a nearby town would not affect its lifestyle in the least. That lifestyle, however, would not be very elaborate. For without the ability to specialize in the production of a particular product, living standards are doomed to some primitive level. Moreover, even the apparent stability from outside disturbances is an illusion. A drought, flood or epidemic affecting our isolated family could easily lead to the ultimate disturbance.

Specialization and trade contribute to greater choice, higher living standards, and provide some insurance from catas-trophe. Economists have long recognized that trade benefits both parties. If it didn't, one of the parties wouldn't trade. However, with trade comes greater exposure to disturbances in other communities. The broader the area of trade, the greater the potential for specialization, and the greater the benefits to all. This is just as true whether the focus is on the relationship between one family and its local community, that community and the rest of the country, or that country and the rest of the world. The political boundaries that surround a nation do not alter the fact that as markets expand, so does the potential for an even greater expansion in living standards.

The impact of international economics on growth and

prosperity stems from the benefits that occur as trade expands to cover greater areas. However, these benefits are no different from those that occur when trade expands within a country. As a result, with respect to its main impact on growth and prosperity, the interaction among economies is nothing more than an extension of the basic principle that the expansion of free trade promotes growth.

Interaction Among Economies—Business Cycles

How does the interaction among economies impact short-term swings in business activity? The answer to this question involves recognizing the distinction between political and economic boundaries and the impact of different currencies. Once these are taken into account, it will be apparent that just as a country's money supply often represents the initiating factor in business cycles, the interaction of monetary policies among countries can introduce an international dimension to those cycles.

Political versus Economic Boundaries

In and of themselves the political boundaries separating one country from another have little economic meaning. These boundaries may or may not be associated with different languages, laws or trade barriers. Even within a given country differences in language, laws or trade barriers may exist. The legal system in Louisiana is different from that of the rest of the United States. This distinction represents a barrier to trade between Louisiana and the other states, but it doesn't make the essence of that state's economic problems one with international dimensions. What does add a distinct economic dimension to any international problem is the use of different currencies.

If all countries had the same currency, then an analysis of how and why one country developed, relative to another, would be equivalent to analyzing how the economy of one state or region within the United States grew, relative to another. Different states or regions are constantly growing faster or slower than the country as a whole. To a certain extent they experience their own regional cycles. So long as the entire country is using the same currency, it should be clear that any differences in growth among the regions results from real economic factors such as an oil discovery or, change in local tax rates.

Real economic factors are constantly changing, both within countries and among countries. As they change, jobs and business opportunities shift from one place to another. When these shifts are in response to changes in real factors, there is no substantive distinction between the adjustments occurring within a country or among countries. People in the Midwest don't like losing job opportunities to the Southwest any more than to Japan. However, when jobs and businesses move to the Southwest it is clear (or should be) that the source of the problem is the deterioration of the economic climate in the Midwest, relative to that of the Southwest. When jobs are lost to Japan or any other country, there is always the possibility that, aside from any change in real factors, the source of the disturbance is somehow related to Japan's monetary policy.

Impact of Different Currencies

Most countries insist upon defining money in terms of their own unique currencies. They also insist upon the power to control the amount of these currencies. At various times some countries have considered it useful to attempt to fix the value of their currency with that of some other country. If this were done perfectly and, say, one U.S. dollar were to equal two German marks, then there would be no more economic difference between one dollar and two marks than between a dollar and a two half dollars.

A perfectly fixed exchange rate between one currency and another transforms the two currencies into one. If this condition were to persist, the relationship between the German economy and the United States, from an economic perspective, would be that of a state to its country. By agreeing to fix the value of one currrency to another, countries agree to a common monetary policy. The only way such an arrangement will work is if one country permits the other to set its monetary policy. In our example, if Germany decided to produce marks at a faster rate than the U.S. was producing dollars, there might be a tendency for the value of the mark to fall. In order to maintain the exchange rate at two marks to a dollar, the U.S. would be forced to produce dollars at a faster pace to maintain the agreed upon rate.

Needless to say, few countries are willing to give up the power and prestige of controlling their own money. Given the desirability of a single currency, efforts to fix exchange rates have been tried time and again. However, just as the U.S. authorities fear that counterfeiters will pollute its money, with fixed exchange rates there is often fear and suspicion that one country may manipulate its money to the detriment of another. When a particular region within a country deteriorates because of an unfavorable local climate, firms and workers will relocate to other regions. Since the entire country has the same monetary policy, local officials in a distressed area cannot logically blame their problems on monetary factors. However, when an individual country experiences the same deterioration in its economic climate, policymakers will seldom stand idly by. The first reaction often is to blame the problem on some other country's monetary policy. A second reaction is to appeal to the government to create more money in an attempt to forestall or minimize the loss of jobs.

On occasion, we hear talk of money crossing a nation's borders. Dollars go abroad, we are told, because foreigners have a greater demand for them; or, they come back to the U.S. because foreigners lose confidence in U.S. policies. Such statements conjure up visions of dollars and bank deposits being loaded onto boats and planes and shipped to foreign countries. In actuality, nothing of the sort occurs. As discussed earlier, money represents a claim to an economy's current output. Dollars represent claims to U.S. output, yen to Japan's output and so on. Except for incidental purposes, these "claims to output" do not leave the country. A particular nation's money is useful only to the extent that it is used to purchase goods and services. And, for the most part, the merchants of each country want to be paid in the currency of that country.

There are exceptions to this tendency. When the value of a country's currency is in doubt or changing rapidly, merchants may temporarily prefer to use another form of money. If dollars were the alternative, there may be a greater demand for U.S. dollars—a demand that has little or no impact on U.S. spending. However, unless the impact is powerful enough to affect the relationship between the growth in U.S. money and the pace of U.S. spending, the argument that money travels from one country to another is a smokescreen that only serves to complicate further an already complex subject.

The actual relationship between the monetary policies of different countries and their impact on business cycles depends on several factors: whether exchange rates between various countries' currencies are allowed to respond to different monetary policies, on the extent of trade between the countries, and on the political reaction within each country. To the extent that currencies are fixed, monetary policies will be similar. As a result, there will tend to be a strong international dimension to the business cycle as economies experience booms and busts related to similar shifts in money. When the exchange rate among currencies is permitted to change in response to market forces, each country has the potential to control its own money, and hence, its own monetary influence over business cycles. However, so long as foreign trade plays a significant role in a country's economy, foreign monetary policy can have an important impact on the domestic economy. A sharp increase in foreign money can lead to a boost in foreign demand, including foreign demand for domestic products. A disturbing cyclical pattern in other countries can lead to wide swings in exchange rates and erratic employment trends in export industries. Finally, these developments can lead to political pressure to alter domestic money policies in an attempt to moderate the changes in currency values and help stabilize the volatility in export-related industries. Hence, the impact of foreign money policies on domestic cycles or on inflation will be as diverse and complex as the number of international monetary arrangements and political responses will allow.

Interaction of Economies—The Value of Money

The value of different currencies depends primarily on what those currencies will buy. And, as discussed in Chapter 12, what they will buy is influenced by the amount of the currency, the rate at which it turns over and the output produced in each country. In addition to these fundamental determinants, the value of one currency in terms of another will be influenced by expectations. Since investors have the option of holding their assets in different currencies, the belief that one currency's value will rise relative to others will cause investors to attempt to acquire that currency to take advantage of the increase. This very process causes the value of the currency to rise, relative to others. As a result, the value of one currency compared with another reflects not only the fundamentals discussed in Chapter 12 but also includes people's expectations of how those fundamentals will change.

By now, another common mistake in economics should be apparent. The mistake occurs when someone suggests that a change in a currency's value will have a particular effect on an economy. The behavior of the dollar, or any other currency, is a *consequence* of many forces, not a *cause*. Without identifying the initiating cause of the change in a currency's value, no meaningful statement can be made about the effects of that change.

For example, many have suggested that a rise in the value of the dollar in terms of foreign currencies will lower U.S. inflation. It is true that the value of the dollar may rise temporarily as a result of a restrictive U.S. monetary policy. And, if the policy lasts for an extended period of time, lower inflation in the U.S. and a rise in the dollar's value would be among the consequences of the slow increases in money. However, the dollar's value may rise for other reasons. Prospects for growth in the U.S. may be improving and investors may attempt to take advantage of this development by buying dollar assets. Alternatively, prospects for growth in other countries may be deteriorating, in which case the dollar's strength will reflect adverse conditions abroad. And finally, the dollar may rise or fall as a result of investors' reassessing their views on the prospects for U.S. economic performance. Such views may be accurate or inaccurate. If they are inaccurate, then the change in the dollar's value is likely to be reversed once the mistake is realized. Each of these various reasons for a change in the value of the dollar will have different implications for the U.S. economy. To ignore the reason for the change in any currency's value and simply to use the change as the starting point in an analysis is a clear example of voodoo analysis.

Another potential source of confusion surrounding the value of money on an international basis stems from the frequent references that are made to a global economy. In such an economy, worldwide supply and worldwide demand combine to set the prices for all internationally traded products. So far, so good. However, it is often stated that worldwide supply and demand combine to produce a world price for a product. And furthermore, that if all such prices are rising, it leads to global inflation. There is nothing wrong with the concept of discussing world money or referring to world prices or world inflation. However, the limited use of such concepts should be recognized.

As an academic exercise, it might be interesting to calculate the impact of world money growth by weighting the growth in different countries' money supplies. Similarly, a weighted average of world inflation might be obtained. However, the usefulness of such concepts is limited. We cannot go to the world stock market or anywhere else to spend our world money. If world inflation happens to be 10 percent a year, the implications for policy or investment strategy are far from clear. If the 10 percent inflation is comprised of rampant inflation in the U.S. and price stability everywhere else, that distinction is crucial. While it is true that we live in a world economy, we do not have a world currency. As a result, any analysis of world markets geared toward policy or investment recommendations should be formulated in terms of a real, live currency.

To a large extent, the same factors that determine growth,

business cycles and the value of money for each economy are at work in the global economy. The use of different currencies is the truly unique factor that distinguishes international economics from any other economics. Different currencies create the potential for different monetary policies and different cyclical movements among countries. As a result, they complicate trade and introduce an important added dimension to the economic process.

Chapter 18

Economic Institutions and Morality

The framework presented in previous chapters can be used to address any number of pressing economic issues. One of the broadest and most important of these is the issue relating to the morality of specific economic policies and of our economic system itself. It is an issue that deserves particular attention in light of the ongoing interest of the clergy in economic affairs.

At one time or another, many of us have questioned the type of economic system that is most consistent with our religious beliefs. Such beliefs call for us to recognize the dignity of all human beings, to help others in every way we can, and to recognize the existence of free will, which, in turn, enables each of us to choose the extent to which our lives will reflect our beliefs. Recently, the U.S. Catholic bishops decided to focus attention on the moral aspects of our free enterprise economic system. Their findings have raised some doubts about the morality of our present system. This, in turn, encourages experimentation with alternative systems. Such experimentation is a serious mistake—a mistake that stems from a failure to understand the dynamics of economics, politics and human nature. The failure to understand these dynamics has been a major factor condemning millions of people around the world to a combination of tyranny, hunger and deprivation.

It is not luck or providence that distinguishes our freedom and prosperity from the tyranny and poverty encountered in so many other countries. Rather, our situation stems in large part from the wisdom of our Founding Fathers. They created a system of political and economic liberty that respects each person as an individual. It is a system that has faith in the choices and decisions of each individual. By so doing, it is a system that maximizes each individual's liberty, maximizes the nation's economic well-being and minimizes its poverty.

Our Founding Fathers were no less concerned with the issues of morality and justice than the most devoutly religious of people. The Founding Fathers' knowledge of economics and politics led them to construct a system that at first blush appears to be crass and amoral, if not outright immoral. However, a deeper understanding of just what they created reveals not only their wisdom concerning economics, but their insights into politics and human nature.

More so than any other, our free enterprise system is extremely complex. Few people have even been able to describe it accurately, no less understand how it operates. Such a description presupposes an understanding of politics, economics, and morality that can easily elude experts in each of these respective fields. And, it is only as the essence of our system is understood that it becomes apparent that it is the only system truly consistent with our fundamental religious beliefs.

Essence of the U.S. Political-Economic System

Whether we refer to our system as free enterprise or use Michael Novak's more descriptive term, democratic capitalism, the essence is the same.[1] From a political perspective, democracy is a system in which important decisions regarding legal rights are determined either directly or indirectly in free elections by the people. From an economic perspective, capitalism refers to a market system characterized by the private ownership of property, in which the individual is free to pursue his commercial interests and reap the rewards and penalties of those decisions.

While there are many dimensions to the wisdom of such a system, two are particularly important. First, political freedom allows for flexibility and dignity. As conditions change, individuals are expected to assess the nature of those changes and determine the extent to which the laws affecting their lives should be altered. Second, economic freedom provides the initiative for individuals to improve their material well-being, the flexibility to make the most efficient use of an economy's resources, the means to provide assistance to others, and, perhaps most important of all, the means to contain the power of the State and the tyranny that can so easily result from such a concentration of power.

Objections to the free enterprise system take many forms. Some point to what appears to be an unjust distribution of wealth or income; others emphasize an apparent waste of resources; and still others focus on the apparent supremacy of commercial values. If we look at the end results of free enterprise, there isn't one of us who can't find something highly objectionable to complain about. However, we have to be careful to determine whether our objections stem from the system or from the behavior of individuals. If the fault lies with the system, then we have every right to try to change it. However, if the fault lies with individuals, then it is the individuals we should try to change, not the system.

Those who believe that their objections lie with the free enterprise system should be aware that a great deal of damage can be brought about by tampering with it. In economics, more so than in any other field, the results of specific policies are often the exact opposite of what we might at first imagine. As a result, ignorance of economics has probably caused more unintentional harm to more people in more places than any other ignorance. It is our responsibility to understand our system completely and to understand the likely impact of any changes in that system before undertaking any serious attempt at reform. What at first blush may appear to be unfair or vulgar may prove to be a result of individual choice and not a result of the system. What at first may appear to be waste or injustice may not be waste or injustice at all, but rather, may reflect the dynamics essential to future development. Or, what may appear to be among the most undesirable of developments may actually result from specific policies or circumstances that are not essential to the system or that actually deviate from the system. Changing the system when the cause lies elsewhere can result in incalculable damage to generations yet to come.

Functions of an Economic System

The first step toward understanding the role of any economic system is to understand what it is that such a system must do. It must develop a way to decide what will be produced with available resources; it must determine how production is to be organized; and it must develop a way to resolve the issue of how income and wealth are to be distributed. Throughout history, there have been only two basic systems for handling these functions—socialism and capitalism. Socialism is an extension of feudalism, where the state or ruler attempts to resolve these issues, while capitalism allows individuals to resolve these issues for themselves.

In practice, no economic system conforms either to pure socialism or to pure capitalism, but many economies have attempted to meld various aspects of each. Even so, we should be aware that calls for government planning represent a call for government to control some combination of the mix of output, the organization of production, or the distribution of income and wealth. And, while it may appear that the potential to help others is more promising when government plays a more active role, appearances can be deceiving. As a result, it's important to understand the essential differences between the two basic economic systems in the entire context of politics, economics and morality.

What Is to Be Produced

In observing the end result of our economic system, none of us can avoid questioning whether the system has either wasted or perverted economic resources. A system that tolerates pet rocks, dog boutiques, punk rock and all the other things to which we might object appears to be frivolously and sinfully wasting resources. However, we have to recognize that any system that maximizes individual freedom and respects the choices of its individuals promotes great diversity. Many of the end products of our economy that I may hate are products you may love. What you deem essential or at least important, I may consider trivial and wasteful.

An economic system has to find a way to resolve these potential conflicts over how resources should be utilized. Under the free enterprise system, individuals are allowed to make their desires known in the marketplace. And, as much as we might disagree with some of the choices, the end products are those things that individuals decided were most important to them, given their available resources.

The alternative to allowing individuals free choice over the direction of economic resources is allowing the State or some other authority to decide such issues. Such a system not only places less faith in individuals' decisions but will also be less tolerant of individual choice. Moreover, the alternative is a system that also must determine who is to make these decisions, and by what criteria. Inevitably, a system that takes this authority from individuals and places it with the State shifts the power structure away from individuals, away from business and commerce, and toward the State. The freedom of individuals to determine what the economy should produce was designed not only to reward individuals for their efforts but to contain the power of the State and the tyranny that such power can produce.

How to Organize Production

Once the issue of what should be produced is resolved there is the crucial issue of how resources should be organized to provide for those goods. In viewing our economic system from the innocent eyes of a child, I thought I had discovered a major flaw. Surely it was a waste of resources to have several gas stations at every busy intersection. I remember thinking, "Who could possibly have made such a wasteful decision?" What I didn't realize at the time was that decisions regarding the number of gas stations and where they should be located were just two of billions upon billions of decisions that had to be made regarding the organization of an economy's resources. Does the economy need more skilled programmers and fewer steel and auto workers? If so, how many? Should products contain more plastic and less metal? If so, how much more? What type of plastic? How should the plastic be made? Should more resources be directed toward machines than research? If so, how much more? What type of machines? The list is seemingly inexhaustible. These are the type of questions that must be answered each day as any economy strives to produce its products through the most efficient use of its resources.

The complexity of this task cannot be overemphasized. Even the smallest firm faces thousands of choices each day regarding materials, workload, and suppliers, as well as countless other issues. Millions of firms are involved in billions of decisions, all in an effort to provide the most efficient use of an economy's resources. To make the problem even more difficult, economies are dynamic. As the relative scarcity of particular resources changes, the correct decisions also change. For an economic system to make efficient use of its available resources, it must find a quick and efficient way to convey information about the relative scarcity of various resources to decisionmakers. Moreover, it must make sure those individuals are aware of any changes in resource availability as soon as possible. And finally, it must instill in its decisionmakers the desire—the motivation—to continually do their best to assure that materials, information, well-trained people and other essential resources are in the right place at the right time.

The free enterprise system solves this problem through the operation of the price system. Prices for millions of products contain all the relevant information necessary for the decisionmaker to assess the relative scarcity of resources. With this information, decisionmakers can determine the most efficient combination of resources for producing any product. When the relative scarcity of any resource changes, so does its price. The new price immediately provides all the information decisionmakers need to reassess the use of other resources. Since the services provided by workers represent an economic resource, wages and salaries must also respond to market pressures so that the relative contribution of particular services can be determined. For those workers with greater responsibilities, wages and salaries will tend to be relatively high. When responsibilities are not fulfilled, workers are replaced and incomes are altered. The combination of responsibility, reward and accountability is what assures the system a continuous supply of conscientious, hard-working individuals who constantly strive for the most efficient use of resources to produce their product.

Under socialism, some or all of the above decisions are made not by individuals, but by the State. To those unfamiliar with the nature of economic systems, the concept of "planning" appears to be an eminently reasonable undertaking. It is. But planning is done in a capitalist economy all the time. Millions of individuals in businesses all across the country are involved in planning for the future. The economic issue surrounding planning is not whether it should be done, but who is to do it. Should it be done by those people directly involved in their business—those who are most affected by its success or failure—or should it be done by the State? If the State is to be involved in planning in a meaningful way, it will have to have more power. For the State to decide that steel production should be 10 percent more than the market needs is meaningless unless the State can enforce that decision. Whatever action the State takes to carry out its plans affects not only those directly involved, but others as well. For it must be able to decide not merely the amount of particular items it wants to see produced, but it must eventually determine the location of plants, the salaries and conditions of workers in those industries and, indirectly, the salaries and conditions of workers in other industries and other areas, as well as what products and materials can move from one location to another and at what price.

When the State engages in economic planning, decisionmakers lose the information contained in the market price of products. Moreover, decisionmakers are no longer rewarded on the basis of their insights to what other people desire or to what combinations of resources are most efficient. Rather, they are rewarded for their ability either to effect political decisions or to anticipate their direction. Under such a system, those who possess political power will be able to direct resources toward the areas they prefer. Those without political power will lose out. Under any system there is always the potential that the power of the State will dominate our lives. Under government planning, there are significant pressures to turn that potential into a reality.

How to Distribute Income and Wealth

Since one of the tenets of our religious beliefs concerns doing everything we can to help others, it appears obvious to some that a redistribution of income from the rich to the poor helps to fulfill that commitment. And what could be easier than using the political system to tax greater portions of the income and wealth of the rich to help alleviate the misery and hunger of the poor? While redistribution of income and wealth may appear to be a straightforward moral issue, it is not. There are important issues surrounding the morality of income redistribution as it pertains to future generations.

Decisions on the distribution of income and wealth can have a major impact on the growth and development of any economy. Taxes on income and wealth can directly discourage productive activity by those affected, can indirectly discourage productive activity from those who might some day be affected, and can reduce the amount of resources directed toward future growth. All of these add up to a system that may redistribute income today by effectively stealing from future generations.

Costs of Economic Systems

The cost of an economic system that ignores market forces, significantly redistributes income, and generally places more power in the hands of the State, can be enormous. At the turn of the century the average income for each person in the United States was a little over $4,000 a year in today's prices. This is similar in magnitude to the average income per person in Mexico today. At the turn of the previous century average income per person in the United States was approximately $2,000, similar in magnitude to today's average income in the Philippines or Thailand. The U.S. economy developed into the most productive, most efficient economy on earth in large part because of its free enterprise system. Development was not smooth or rapid. It was painstakingly slow, with increases in per capita income averaging only 1 to 1½ percent per year. There's no magical, overnight formula for development. It takes time, patience and an economic system that places its faith and confidence in the decisions and abilities of its people. Under such a system, continuing efforts to achieve an efficient use of resources lead to a significant improvement in living standards from one generation to the next. With this improvement comes the greatest potential to help others who are less fortunate.

It's interesting to note that many generations ago the leaders in Latin America applied a different political-economic model than the one used by our Founding Fathers. The economic model applied to Latin America was similar to the one used in Spain and Portugal. It was a model where the Church and State played a dominant role. Business and commerce were held in low esteem. In the end, Latin America's economies did not develop and grow as did the economy of the United States. Rather, economic stagnation and generation after generation of poverty have characterized these economies. There is nothing socially or morally redeeming about a stagnant economy.

Efforts on the part of the clergy to make relevant statements about the morality of economic systems are not new. Given the important role of the clergy in society, those statements can have a major impact on a country's development. Adam Smith, who accurately projected the miracle of economic development in the United States, was particularly critical of the clergy of his day. He pointed out that in Spain and Portugal, as well as in the countries of Latin America, where the clergy had a great deal of influence, the potential for development was being hampered. To the extent that Smith's observation is accurate, the lack of economic development and resulting poverty found in Latin America today is attributable, at least in part, to a clergy that failed to grasp some critical lessons in economics. Had the same theological force held sway over the political-economic development of the United States, the strife, misery and poverty found in so many other countries, would likely be found in our own as well.

Morality, Free Enterprise and the Role of the Clergy

It's interesting to note that all of the great economists who promote the free enterprise system—Adam Smith, Friedrich Hayek, Milton Friedman—emphasize its implications for improving the lot of mankind. Their overriding objective in supporting such a system is to promote economic development and provide higher living standards and greater opportunities for advancing the condition of the poor. Interestingly, all the great promoters of free enterprise believe that a redistribution of income should be an integral part of the system. Sharing the bounty of a successful economy with those less fortunate or less able to care for themselves is a fundamental, humanitarian goal that must exist in any truly successful society. What is objectionable is to redistribute income to such an extent that the economy's future development and prosperity are impaired.

It surprises some to find that the greatest defenders of the free enterprise system support government efforts to improve the environment, to develop a system of social services to help the needy, and to regulate business. What is objectionable is how these programs are carried out. In order to be consistent with the most efficient use of resources, markets must be free to adjust and competition must thrive. The influence of government in markets must be held to a minimum. So long as prices and commodities are free to adjust, resources can be utilized efficiently. So long as restrictions or regulations affect all equally, they may well be consistent with a healthy economy. However, when taxes or regulations stifle development, when the State plans for individuals, or when ill-defined welfare programs condemn its recipients to a continuous state of poverty, the "fairness" or "justice" of these policies has to be reconsidered.

In the course of the 1960s, Great Britain moved its economy toward socialism with state ownership of private industry, socialized medicine, an elaborate social-welfare system, and high rates of taxation—all based on concepts of equality, equity, and a "fair" distribution of wealth. Just as Adam Smith would have predicted, the results were disastrous. Great Britain went from one of the world's leading nations, characterized by widespread prosperity, to a nation torn by internal dissent and rapidly falling living standards. By the mid-1970s, of all the leading nations of the world, only the Soviet Union had a less productive economy than Great Britain.

In the United States, similar efforts to tax the rich, redistribute wealth, and have the State provide jobs and protect individuals from their own decisions, have had a similar impact. For the first time in modern economic history, the end of the 1970s was characterized by a sharp decline in the average worker's living standard and a so-called malaise that spread through the nation. To some, the cure for this malaise appeared obvious. They would give even more power to the State to provide individuals with even greater protection from their own choices and greater security from the apparent uncertainties of a competitive environment. In addition, they would produce an even more confiscatory tax system. From a historical perspective, such policies provide transitory help to some at the expense of others while condemning future generations to the type of strife, turmoil and tyranny that is sure to accompany such moves.

Fortunately, a major change in the direction of economic policies was undertaken in the United States in the early 1980s. The role of government in solving specific economic problems was reduced and tax rates were cut substantially. In the years that followed, productivity and living standards once again began to rise, job opportunities expanded at an astounding pace and the performance of the U.S. economy once again became the showcase for the rest of the world.

There are a great many important moral issues facing a free enterprise economy. Given its efficiency in utilizing economic resources to raise living standards, it would seem obvious that the people who reap such benefits have a moral obligation to help others. By making individuals more aware of the plight of those less fortunate than ourselves, and by reminding people of their moral obligation to help others, the clergy might well be able to do a better job of immediately reducing suffering, poverty and hunger. However, to reduce the poverty and hardship faced by future generations, the clergy will find that it's necessary to promote an economic system that encourages the most efficient use of economic resources— one that has a proven record in its past and one that is most likely to minimize poverty, hunger and tyranny for generations to come. Such a system is the one created by our Founding Fathers. They had faith in the ability of individuals to make the right choices, and so strove to minimize the role of the State in deciding what should be produced, how it would be produced and who would reap the appropriate economic rewards and penalties. Such a system has the utmost respect for individuals, and, as a result, is the one that is most consistent with respecting human dignity. Given its ability to utilize resources efficiently and its success in raising living standards, it provides the maximum potential for helping others. What is needed is not to change our economic system so that individuals end up less able to help either others or themselves. What is needed is to impress upon individuals the moral obligations that accompany their freedom and prosperity.

Book 4

Wrapping
It All Up

Chapter 19

Conclusion

In traversing the economic landscape, we have covered a great deal of territory, territory that too often is strewn with mines and potholes. The objective has been a simple one—to provide a helpful guide to a confusing and, at times, hostile environment. In attempting to do so we often poked fun at many of the economic views that are frequently encountered, playfully admonishing the more obvious mistakes as voodoo.

As with many journeys, the first step in this one is the most important. That step—establishing a structure for organizing issues and information—cannot be overemphasized. Too often, a weak or faulty structure becomes the single most important source of economic voodoo. Once the structure is developed, issues must be clearly defined, theories or explanations chosen and evidence evaluated.

Even with the best structure, numerous pitfalls will arise. Several guiding principles for avoiding the more obvious of these include identifying the major initiating force that explains a particular issue, tracing the impact of that force through the economy and being familiar with the historical foundations for explaining various issues.

The final step in our efforts at voodoo busting is to observe. To attain a working knowledge of economics is a process without end. Regardless of what has been accomplished to date, much remains to be learned. And the key to further progress is observation. Observe how people react to changing circumstances. Observe how conditions change with different policies. For it's only by becoming immersed in the actions, adventures, and mishaps of the real world that economics can truly be understood. In the end, such immersion may prove to be the most effective way to distill the voodoo from economics once and for all.

About the Author

Robert J. Genetski is currently Senior Vice President and Chief Economist at Chicago's Harris Bank. He also serves as the George F. Bennett visiting Professor of Economics at Wheaton College. He is the author, along with Beryl Sprinkel (Chairman of President Reagan's Council of Economic Advisers), of the book *Winning With Money* and has authored many pioneering articles on the effect of tax rates on economic performance. Dr. Genetski's articles have appeared in *Fortune Magazine, The Wall Street Journal* and numerous other periodicals. His undergraduate training was at Eastern Illinois University and he received his Ph.D. in Economics from New York University. Dr. Genetski has taught economics at both New York University and at the University of Chicago's Graduate School of Business.

Footnotes and Sources

Chapter 3

[1]Hymans, Saul H., "Saving, Investment and Social Security," *The National Tax Journal*, March 1981, p. 7.

[2]Roberts, Paul Craig, "Mr. Feldstein's Fiscal Folly," *Wall Street Journal*, June 1, 1983, p. 28.

[3]Dewald, William G., "Deficits and Monetary Growth," Federal Reserve Bank of Atlanta, *Economic Review*, January, 1984, p. 18.

Chapter 5

[1]Gilder, George, *Wealth and Poverty* (New York: Basic Books, Inc., 1981) pp. 47-63.

[2]Duncan, Greg J., *Years of Poverty and Years of Plenty* (Michigan: The University of Michigan, 1984) p. 40.

[3]*Ibid.,* pp. 64-74.

Chapter 6

[1]Hayek, Friedrich A., *The Road to Serfdom* (Chicago: The University of Chicago Press, 1944) pp. 48-50).

[2]Smith, Adam, *An Inquiry Into the Nature and Causes of The Wealth of Nations* (New York: Random House, Inc., Modern Library Edition, 1937, originally published in 1776) pp. 423, 534-38, 541.

[3]*Ibid.,* p. 590.

[4]Friedman, Milton and Rose, *Free to Choose* (New York: Avon Books, 1979) p. xvii.

[5]*Ibid.,* pp. 25-26.

[6]*Ibid.,* pp. 49-55.

[7]*Ibid.,* pp. 47-49.

[8]*Ibid.,* p. 53.

[9]*Ibid.*

[10]*Ibid.*

[11]Hayek, *op. cit.,* p. xx.

Chapter 7

[1]Smith, Adam, *op. cit.,* pp. xliii, 433, 439, 529, 583, 625, 778-79 and 800.

[2]George, Henry, *Protection or Free Trade* (New York: The Schalkenback Foundation, 1980, originally published in 1886) p. 168-169.

[3]George, Henry, *Progress and Poverty* (New York: The Schalkenback Foundation, 1979, originally published in 1879) p. 434.

[4]Calvin Coolidge as quoted in Wanniski, Jude, *The Way the World Works* (New York: Basic Books, Inc., 1978) pp. 131-32.

[5]Price Waterhouse, *Individual Taxes—A Worldwide Summary* (1984 Edition) pp. 99-101.

[6]Keleher, Robert E., "Supply-Side Economics: Guiding Principles for the Founding Fathers," Federal Reserve Bank of Atlanta, *Economic Review*, September, 1982, pp. 42-53.

[7]Wanniski, Jude, *op. cit.,* pp. 127-159 and 258.

[8]Pan, Enlin, "Marginal Tax Rates: Methodology," Harris Bank Research Report, March 9, 1981.

[9]Genetski, Robert J., "The Impact of Marginal Tax Rates on U.S. Productivity Performance," Testimony before the Senate Subcommittee on Oversight of the Internal Revenue Service of the Finance Committee, Washington, D.C., April 13, 1984.

Chapter 8

[1]Malthus, Thomas Robert, *Essay on Population,* as reprinted in *Classics of Economic Theory,* edited by George W. Wilson (Bloomington: Indiana University Press, 1964), p. 164.

[2]Smith, Adam, *op. cit.,* p. 643.

[3]Marx, Karl, *Capital,* as reprinted in *Classics, op. cit.,* p. 385.

[4]Thurow, Lester C., *The Zero-Sum Society,* (New York: Basic Books Inc., 1980), p. 6.

[5]*Ibid.,* pp. 8-9.

[6]*Ibid.,* p. 11.

[7]*Ibid.,* p. 77.

[8]Marx, *op. cit.,* p. 384.

[9]Thurow, *op. cit.,* p. 79.

Chapter 10

[1]Hume, David, *Political Discourses* (Edinburgh: A. Kincaid and A. Donaldson, 1752) p. 47. Thornton, Henry, *An Equiry Into the Nature and Effects of the Paper Credit of Great Britain (1802)* (New York: Farrar & Rinehart Inc., 1939) pp. 236-237. Mises, Ludwig von, *The Theory of Money and Credit* (Indianapolis: Library Classics, 1980, originally published in 1912) p. 157.

[2]*Ibid.,* p. 168.

[3]Friedman, Milton and Schwartz, Anna, *A Monetary History of the United States, 1867-1960* (Princeton, New Jersey: Princeton University Press, 1963), pp. 686-695.

Chapter 11

[1]Samuelson, Paul A. and Norhaus, William D., "A Grander Role for Money Policy," *The New York Times,* February 17, 1985, Section 3, p. 10.

[2]Keynes, John Maynard, *The General Theory of Employment, Interest, and Money* (New York: Harcourt, Brace & World, Inc., 1964, originally published in 1935), pp. 141, 313 and 317.

[3]Hayek, Friedrich A., "The Keynes Centenary: The Austrian Critique" *The Economist,* June 11, 1983, p. 39.

[4]*Ibid.*

[5]Friedman, Milton, "The Keynes Centenary: A Monetarist Reflects" *The Economist,* June 11, 1983, p. 19.

Chapter 12
[1]Petty, Sir William, *Quantulumcunque Concerning Money, 1682,* in *The Economic Writings of Sir William Petty,* ed. by Charles Henry Hull (New York: Augustus M. Kelly, 1964) pp. 439, 442 and 446.
[2]*Wall Street Journal,* January 24, 1984, p. 1.

Chapter 13
[1]Vilar, Pierre, *A History of Gold and Money 1450-1920* (London: Atlantic Highlands: Humanities Press, 1976) p. 163, 182, 191, 209, and 217-218.
[2]*Ibid.,* p. 183.
[3]*Ibid.,* p. 189-191.
[4]Hume, David, *op. cit.,* p. 47.
[5]Thorton, Henry, *op. cit.,* p. 197.
[6]Mises, Ludwig von, *op. cit.,* p. 177.
[7]Keynes, John Maynard, *op. cit.,* p. 309.
[8]*Economic Report of the President* Transmitted to the Congress January, 1981 (Washington: United States Government Printing Office, 1981) p. 43.

Chapter 14
[1]Sprinkel, Beryl W. and Genetski, Robert J. *Winning With Money* (Homewood, Illinois: Dow Jones-Irwin, 1977) pp. 99-101.

Chapter 15
The primary source for this chapter is Fisher, Irving, *The Nature of Capital and Income* (New York: The Macmillan Co., 1930, originally published in 1906).

Chapter 16
The primary source for this chapter is Fisher, Irving, *The Rate of Interest* (New York: Garland Publishing, Inc. 1982, originally published in 1907).

Chapter 17
The primary source for this chapter is Iverson, Carl, *International Capital Movements* (New York: Augustus M. Kelley, 1967, originally published in 1935).

Chapter 18
Many of the ideas for this chapter stem from Michael Novak's book, *The Spirit of Democratic Capitalism,* (New York: Simon and Schuster, 1982) which is destined to become a classic in the field of morality and economcs. In addition, those wishing to delve deeper into this important topic should refer to Milton Friedman's *Capitalism and Freedom;* Friedrich A. Hayek's *The Road to Serfdom;* Adam Smith's *Wealth of Nations;* and George Gilder's *Wealth and Poverty.*